Small Houses in Nature

Edition 2006

Author: Arian Mostaedi
Editorial Coordinator: Jacobo Krauel
Graphic designer & production: Dimitris Kottas
Text: contributed by the architects, edited by Amber Ockrassa

© Carles Broto i Comerma
Jonqueres, 10, 1-5
08003 Barcelona, Spain
Tel.: +34 93 301 21 99
 Fax: +34-93-301 00 21
E-mail: info@linksbooks.net
www. linksbooks.net

Small Houses in Nature

index

introduction

Architecture is the discipline that deals with space: it works in space, from and with space. From an architectural point of view, this conditioning element is becoming increasingly scarce and paradoxically, the scarcer it is the more important its role in a project. The organization and optimization of space reveal an architect´s skill in response to the challenges of a limited space, a small site or a reduced budget. In this sense, architecture has been able to reinvent itself over and over, through the new construction and technological advances that appear on an almost daily basis. The idea of the primate "refuge", present at the gestation period of all small housing projects, leads into infinite dwelling possibilities that trancend the actual space and area available. Spatial optimization expands into the fields of versatility and the multifunctionality of constructive elements, including furnishing and instalations.

This book provides a sampling of this ongoing architectural redefinition: an overview of rural, traditional and experimental, weekend and permanent houses. In all their manifestations, they show that in architecture, reduced and compact doesn´t necessarily mean "limited".

This extensively documented book presents complete detailed technical and graphic information for each project and its design process, from conception to completition. The internationally recognized architects contribute additional information and details of the solution adopted in each case. This combination provides a wide range of suggestions and useful examples that can help to define future projects. In short, an invaluable tool for all kinds of professionals and students of architecture and interior design.

Gert & Karin Wingårdh

The Millhouse

Photographs: James Silverman

Göteborg, Sweden

This delightful structure, designed through the collaboration of Gert and Karin Wingårdh, is a unique fusion of east-meets-west. Measuring only 538 sqft (50 m²), it makes a statement through simple architectural language and integration with the surroundings. The Millhouse is Wingardh's unique translation of Frank Lloyd Wright's principles of incorporating geographical and botanical elements and blending smooth materials with natural elements, just one example being rough boulders left in place in the floor. A contemporary interpretation of a traditional Japanese tea house, the structure seems to be floating on the water. Wingårdh redirected the water from the stream to an outdoor bathtub, which then overflows onto the limestone platform and trickles down into a reflecting pool.

If the grounds are eloquent, the house echoes the experience but with a distinctive twist. With high ceilings, simple, expressive materials, and walls of clear glass sliding doors, the house enjoys an integral relationship with nature. Oak and limestone are used with precise craftsmanship, emphasizing the formal simplification of the space.

Upon entering, the eye takes in the whole ground floor in one sweep. The floor plan is unencumbered by walls, yet each space is distinctive within its own defined area. Limestone flooring connects the interior spaces and continues beyond the glass walls as an extension of the living area. The main structural support system is a steel T-column, which has been left exposed to rust. The T-beam supports the load of the smooth oak beams resting on it. Two walls of frameless glass doors contribute to the design solution of creating the perception of a larger space.

The interior detailing is a collaboration of Gert's and Karin's design skills, with Karin custom designing the furniture, which is mostly in American maple and constructed in a jigsaw manner without the use of nails.

Adhering to the "work triangle" concept, the floor plan of the kitchen creates fluid circulation between the three main points: from the stove, to the sink and refrigerator, then back. Appliances and supplies are concealed in the cabinet doors, freeing up the kitchen from clutter.

Up a flight of stairs located at the back of the kitchen, the bedroom is a simple, appealing area set under an A-frame ceiling. Long horizontal boards on the walls help accent the length of the room, while vertical boards behind the bed provide the perception of height.

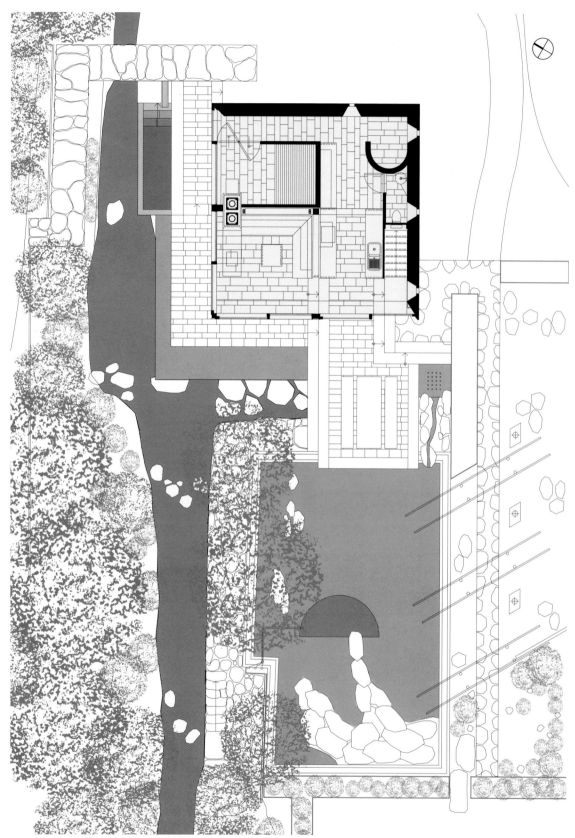

Reminiscent of the early work of Frank Lloyd Wright, an inspiration to Wingårdh, the use of cantilevered limestone slabs under the residence and over the water is an ingenious way to merge the house with the gardens.

A limestone slab is cantilevered over the reflecting pool so that there is a constant trickling sound of water cascading off the ledges. The interior flooring extends to the exterior, merging the living space with the natural space outside.

Site plan

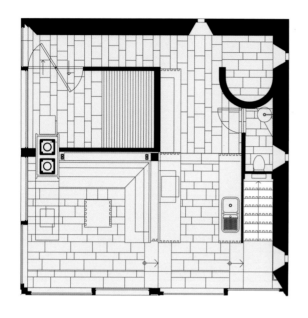

Ground floor

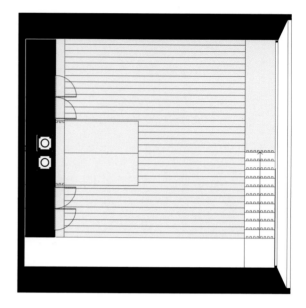

First floor

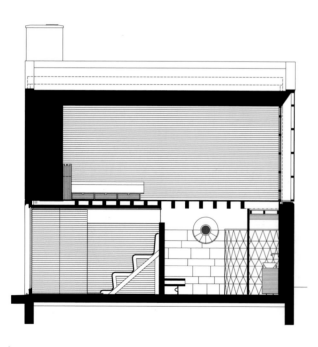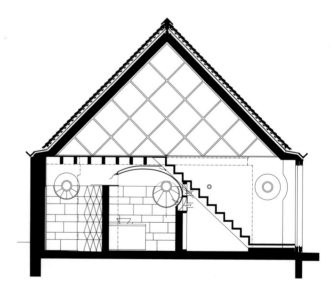

Sections

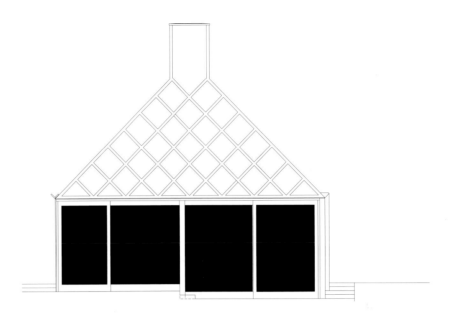

North elevation

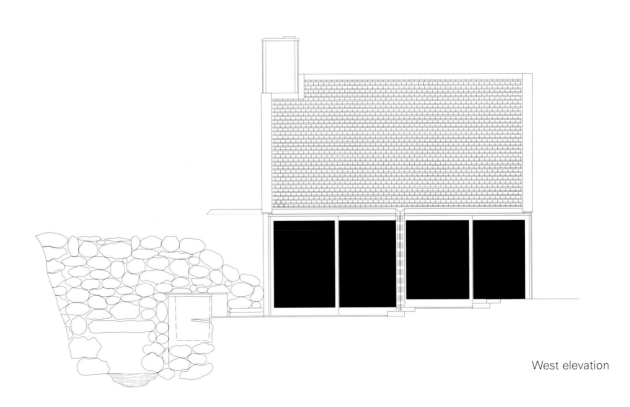

West elevation

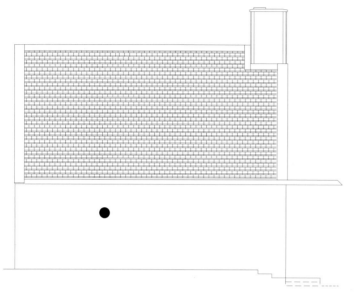

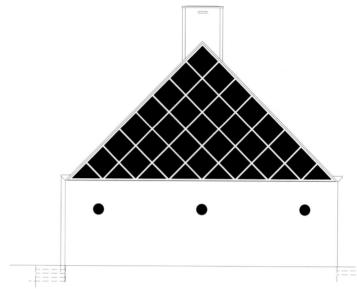

East elevation

South elevation

The built in furnishings, designed by Karin Wingård, feature dovetail joints that are also used on the counters and stairs, showing that great craftsmanship does not require the use of nails.

A small toilet off the kitchen is divided from the shower area by this gentle curving wall. The curved ceiling section above the vanity mimics the curve of the wall.

The bath and sauna entrance illustrates the beautiful incorporation of limestone and oak. The stone wall outside assures privacy for the sauna, while the glass wall allows for natural lighting and a view of nature.

Todd Saunders & Tommie Wilhelmsen

Summer House
(2 of 3- a series of summer houses)

Photographs: contributed by Saunders & Wilhelmsen Arkitekter AB   Hardanger Fiord, Norway

This is our own personal project. We bought this site ourselves in order to create experimental architecture. The constant question for young architects was how to find clients willing to take a chance on enthusiastic architects with little experience? When we first started our firm, instead of going and looking for clients we went looking for a possible site to build an experimental structure. In this way we could pursue our architectural vision in line with our convictions: no compromises, original, and respecting the Norwegian landscape that we live in. Once we made such a project, we knew that it would be easier to find and convince clients that we are competent architects through this use of a real life building as opposed to paper visions of architecture so common among young architects.

We found a site about 2 hours drive from Bergen in Hardanger, on the edge of one of Norway's most dramatic fjords. We bought this site with all of our savings. We made a structure that would be a part of the natural surroundings, yet in a sensitive contrast to the dramatic landscape. We divided this retreat into two parts: one for the function of eating and sleeping and another smaller room that could be used for whatever the user desired. A long thin floating outdoor deck connects these two parts and makes the space twice as large in the summer, and one can walk barefoot from one to the other. The front of this arrangement faces the fjords, but the inner space towards the mountain creates an evening space that can be complemented by a small fire.

We built both structures ourselves together with a carpenter. We are now just finishing the smaller building of the two projects. In June we will start constructing the second longer structure. This longer structure will be finished in July The house is quite environmental in that it is insulated with recycled newspapers and all trees are conserved and integrated into the project.

The project will be used as a retreat for friends and ourselves during the next year. It will be a place where one can disconnect. The intention is to have minimalist interiors and the least possible technology. Any technology will be supported by natural gas. We hope to use candles as the natural light source. This part of Norway only has about 4 hours darkness in the summer month, the time of year this retreat will be used the most.

When one sits on the large outdoor deck the views are almost hypnotising. The site has a church-like feeling to it, with the darker forest in the back, but with a large open light in front. The mountains, the clouds, and the fiord are constantly making subtle changes through the day, that one can sit and be fascinated by.

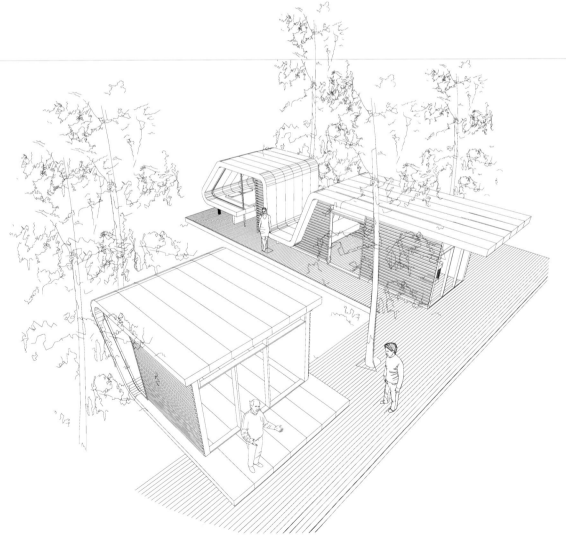

When one sits on the large outdoor deck the views are almost hypnotising. The site has a church-like feeling to it, with the darker forest in the back, but with a large open light in front. The mountains, the clouds, and the fiord are constantly making subtle changes through the day, that one can sit and be fascinated by.

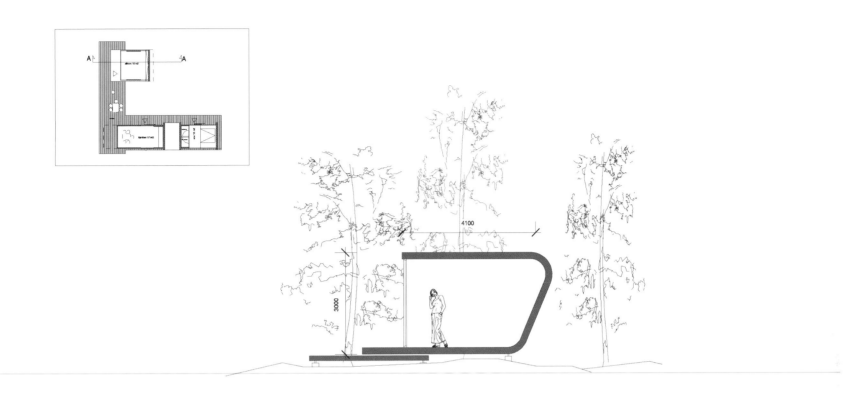

This is the nearest one is permitted to build to the waterside. All new architecture has to be at least 100m from the shoreline. We had to apply for special permission to build 80m from the shore. The retreat is approximately 80m above sea level, making for a dramatic relationship to the large fjord in front. On the western side of the site, approximately 30m from the cabin, there are 30m high waterfalls in the Forrest that continues in a dramatic stream. One crosses this stream on the up the cabin over an old stone foot bridge.

Daigo Ishii + Future-scape

Cottage in Kawanishi

Photographs: Future Scape and Japan Architect

Kawanishi, Japan

This cottage is located in the region of Japan that receives the greatest amount of annual snowfall, which is sometimes as deep as four meters. At the same time, summer temperatures might soar as high as 38° C (100° F) and are usually accompanied by an uncomfortably high level of humidity. Such climatic conditions inevitably became determining forces in the design of this home in the woods.

Local architectural tradition necessarily formed the basis for the external shape of the building, especially the roof, with its sharp ridge and steep slope to prevent a dangerous accumulation of heavy snow. Furthermore, the ridge is exactly in the centerline of the roof to ensure an equal distribution on either side of snow. The overhang of the eaves has been kept as short as possible to ensure that as snow melts in the spring and piles up at the lower end of the roof plane, it will be well supported by the load-bearing walls of the structure.

Another determining factor in the shape of the cottage was the budget, with this simple rectangle occupying the largest possible volume. The wide, open spaces of the interior were needed to create a comfortable degree of air flow during the hot, humid summer months.

The end result of these combined functions is referred to by the architect as "Black Box, White Tube". The black box is the basic shape, and is plainly seen as such even from the inside, surrounding the negative spaces leftover from the "white tube". The white tube, enclosed in slip-boarded dividing walls, is a row of volumes housing the home's essential functions (bathrooms, bedrooms, kitchen, etc.). However, rather than being placed in a straight row, the restricted length of the house has resulted in a bent and jumbled "row" which guarantees the maximum degree of space for each function.

A traditional vernacular was used on the exterior in order to keep its external look in line with the other homes in the area and so as not to aesthetically compete with the surrounding beech woods. However, the impression changes radically on the inside, with an unexpected juxtaposition of shapes and tones in a purely contemporary idiom.

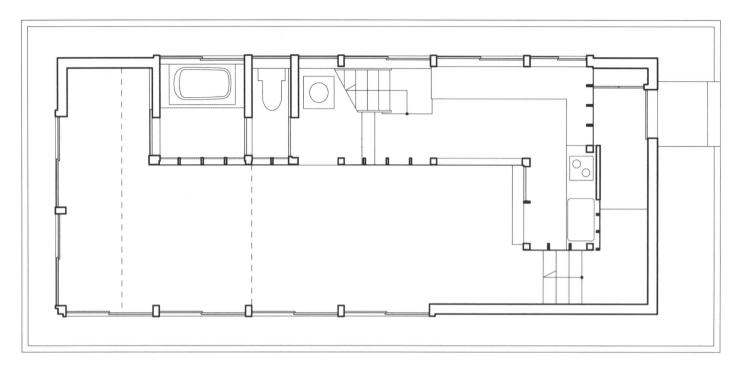

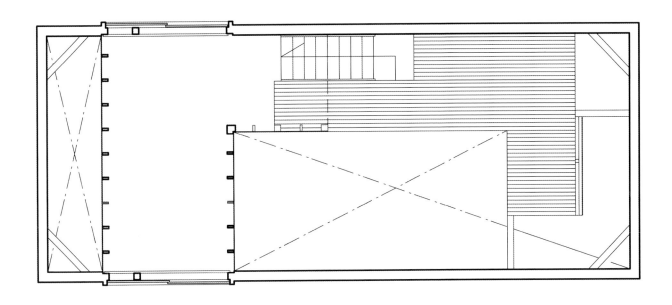

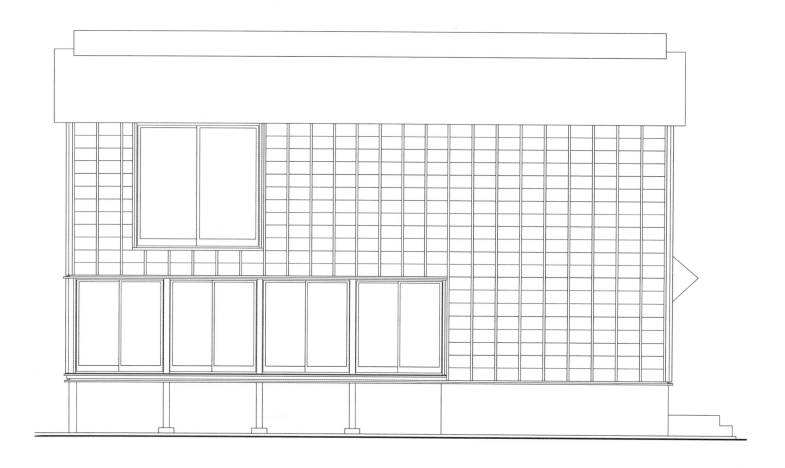

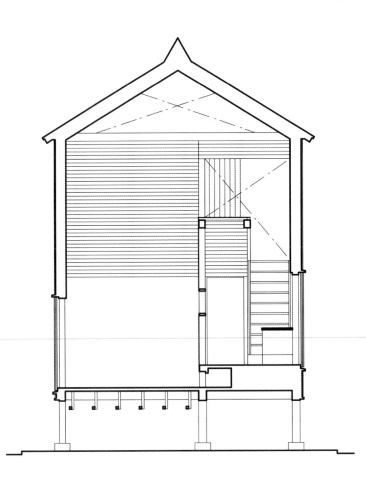

Gap between the two volumes: Black Box and White Cube

Black Box

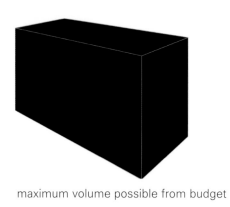

maximum volume possible from budget

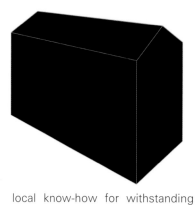

local know-how for withstanding heavy snow

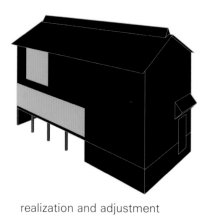

realization and adjustment

White Tube

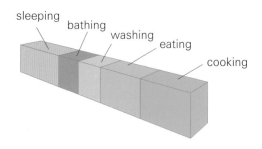

sleeping
bathing
washing
eating
cooking

essential living functions

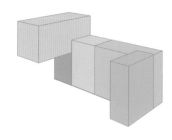

bent by the restriction of Black Box

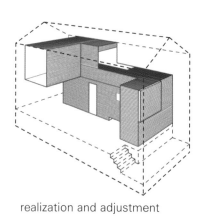

realization and adjustment

A traditional vernacular was used on the exterior in order to keep its external look in line with the other homes in the area and so as not to aesthetically compete with the surrounding beech woods. However, the impression changes radically on the inside, with an unexpected juxtaposition of shapes and tones in a purely contemporary idiom.

GD Architectes FAS SIA
Mountain Cabin

Photographs: Thomas Jantscher

Praz-De-Fort, Switzerland

Looking like a barn, this minimalist house stands on posts and looks as if it were suspended on the high plain of Saleina. A reinterpretation of the traditional beam-and-post construction, built of wooden panels of the same arboreal species, providing the structure, the insulation and the finish material of the spaces. The unity of the material settles the alpine character of this contemporary construction.

Reflecting on a programme of holiday homes allows us to rethink the organisation, the configuration and the size/dimensions of the living area. The ground floor is made up of a space of 9.84 x 39.36 ft (3 x 12 m), which includes living room/dinning room/ kitchen and a large terrace as an outside room which extends the habitation. The first floor has 4 minimal sized bedrooms (7.87x9.84ft, 2,40x3,00m). In the north, the layout of the distribution contains the sanitary facilities and the settings.

Trying to develop a chalet in a modern way allows us to rethink the relationship with the landscape. Also, the bay window on the ground floor extends the space of the living room up towards the slope of the wooded hill situated opposite, the opening of the parents bedroom window fits with the bell tower of Portalet church, and the horizontal glass work of this space makes the view over the valley into a living picture.

This care to associate the landscape and architecture is further reinforced by the formalization of the terrace and the work surface of the kitchen. Both of which add to the expression of the cabin projecting the user to the outside. This feeling is maintained by the relationship of these two elements with the main volume.

Looking at it from a constructive point of view, three months were needed for the completion of this project. This construction time includes the prefabrication in the workshop, the assembly on site as well as all the interior finishing.

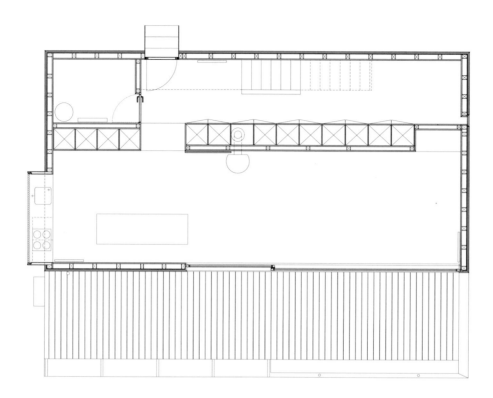

Ground floor

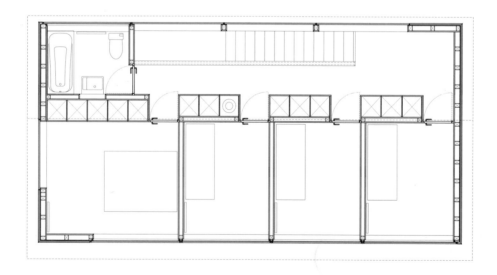

First floor

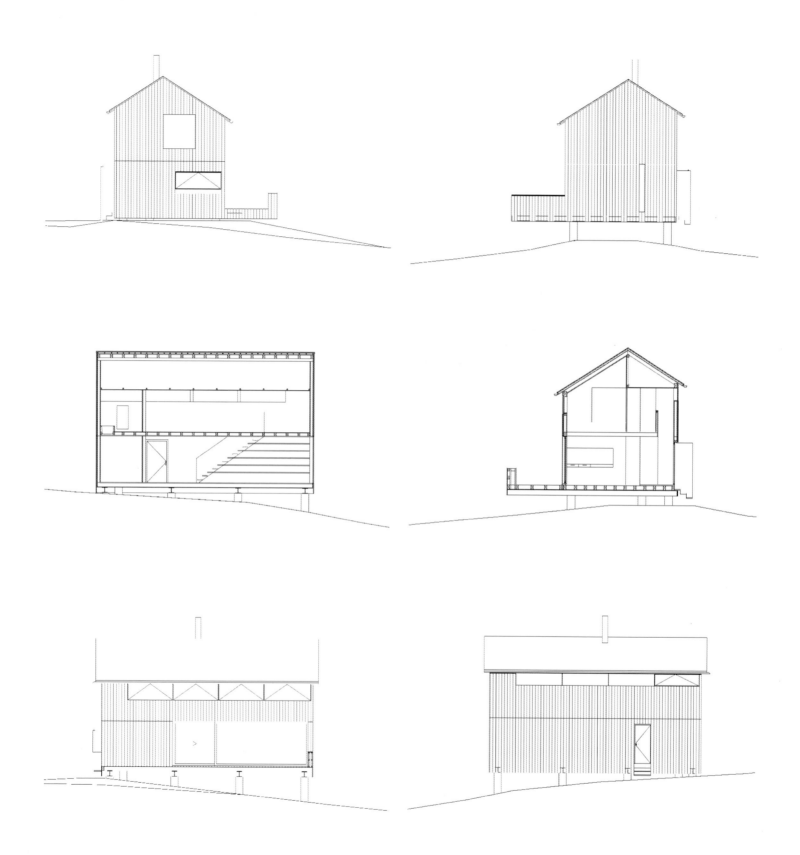

Schmidt, Hammer & Lassen / Bjarne Hammer
A resort for holiday

Photographs: Larsenform.com

Juelsminde, Jutland, Denmark

This holiday home is sited at Juelsminde in Jutland, ensconced in a wooded area at the tip of a promontory, just minutes' walking distance from north- and south-facing beaches. When the family bought the land the only structures on it were a couple of shacks, so modest in size that, tucked up in their bunk beds at night, they could tell each other stories while the wind whistled through the treetops. The experience of those shared days of living together in a small chalet set amid the pristinity of nature sparked the idea of a new cottage that would replace the old.

The cottage comprises two rectangular volumes (904 sqft): a larger communal dwelling complemented by an annex that virtually abuts it. Both volumes are designed as frames that allow light and space to stream through the open and extensively glazed long sides - timber casings of the cottage's functions and of the vistas that present themselves to the viewer looking through the house.

Beneath the roof and spanning its twin gables, the larger structure features the cottage's expansive high-ceilinged living space: a freestanding kitchen, a dining- and living area plus patio.

The larger building's two long sides face southwest and northwest, respectively, and are basically wide open to the landscape. To the southwest, eleven identical perpendicular panels of glass span ceiling and floor, yielding a trans-parent façade that opens up with ease. The cottage's occupants thus enjoy the amenity of being able to step straight out onto the patio along the entire length of the living area. The kitchen, a rectangular concrete unit, extends from the body of the cottage out onto the patio - accentuating the fact that here indoor activities blend into outdoor ones.

On the opposite side of the communal living space, the smaller unit is punched into the larger building's northwest-facing glass façade. Set against the extensive glazing of the cottage proper, the annex presents itself as a detached and independent volume.

Moreover, the annex delivers the cottage's functional axis, as defined by compactly integrated spaces: three alcove-style bedrooms featuring twin bunk beds with immediate and open access to the main building, and separated from the natural environment only by glazing, a feature that also marks the bathroom/toilet facilities, and cupboard niches. A quartet of small gates means that the children can step outside from each of the three alcoves as well as from the bathroom area.

The annex has a floor level one step up from the main building - a slight counterpoint to what is otherwise an immediate transition from the capaciousness of the main building to the sleeping quarters of the smaller.

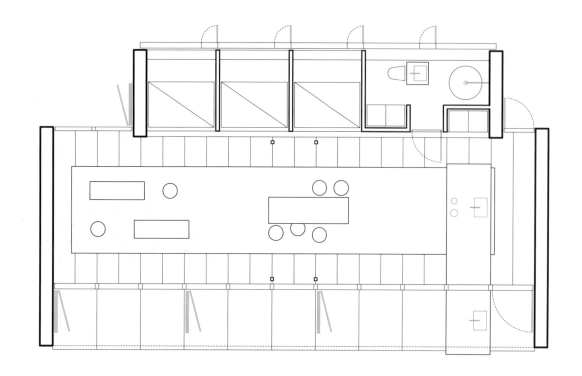

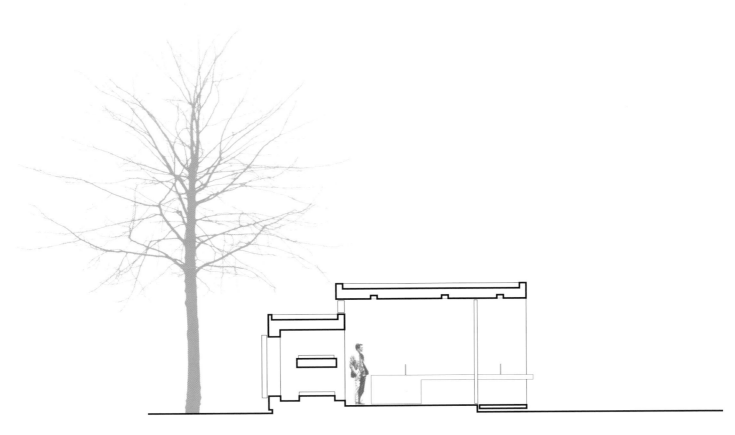

On every dimension, to minimize as far as possible the disjunction between inside and out, and thereby achieve a pervasive simplicity. To reduce the total square meters within and thereby gain an infinitely greater world outside. To keep the furnishings spare and thereby sharpen our awareness of each other, the flow of conversation, the impact of the view and the subtle nuances of the changing light.

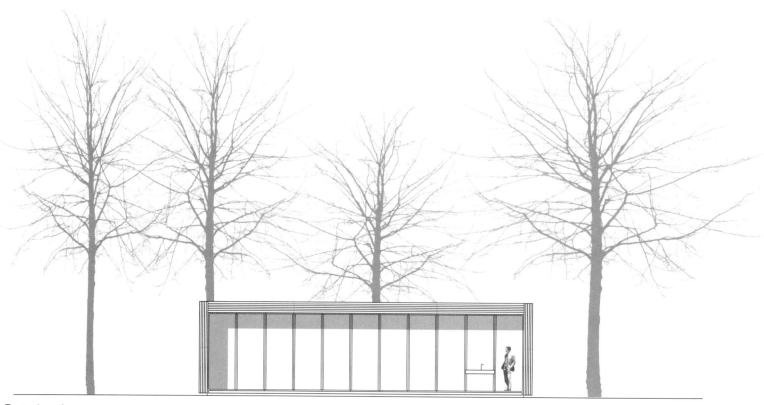

East elevation

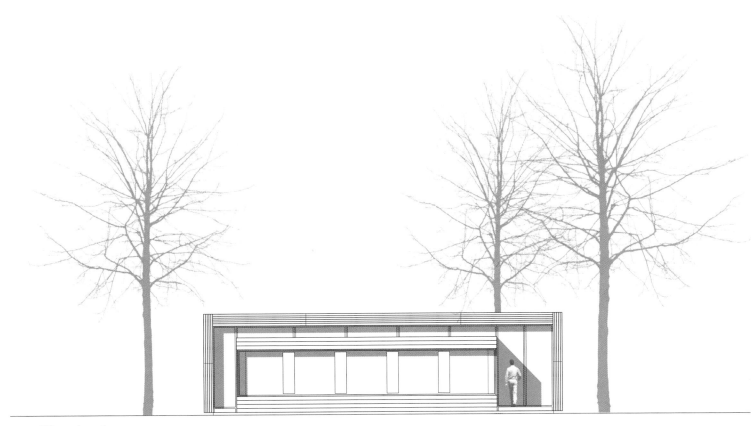

West elevation

Standing on the lawn outside the house, it is easy to get a clear sense of the cottage's informing idea. A Nordic summer evening, a deep blue sky topping the forest canopy - the large glass panels slid away and people relaxing on the patio, sitting at the long table. Beyond them, the annex's structure of tightly-integrated intimate spaces and, framing the whole, a density of green foliage.

Timber and glass preponderate. Slats and cladding in Siberian larch offer, inside and out, vertical and horizontal profiles, respectively - a refinement of the materiality of the wood, the summer cottage as wooden casket. Glass set in vertical frames of Oregon pine secures the open aspect. In conjunction with the rough-coated light-toned concrete of the kitchen table, the area of polished concrete flooring that in the main unit complements the wooden flooring offsets the warm accents of the timber.

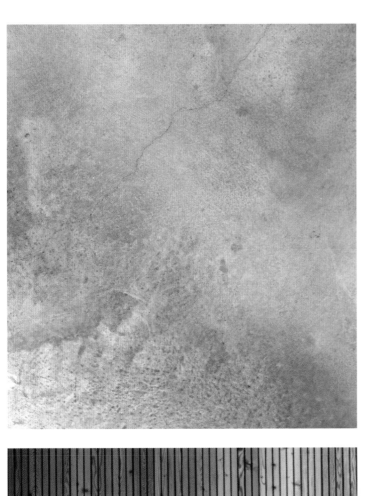

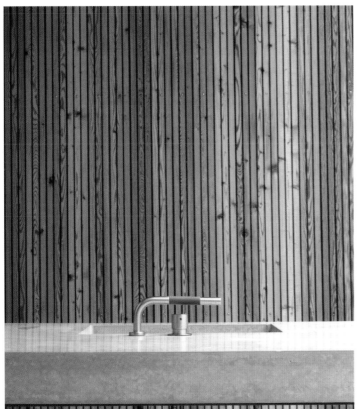

Tommie Wilhelmsen

Parcell Garden Stavanger

Photographs: Nils Petter Dale

Stavanger, Norway

This small cabin, its living area measuring just 258 sqft (24m²) was built by the architect himself with the help of a handsaw and a hammer. It is sited on one of approximately 200 other garden parcels, each measuring 2152 sqft (200 m²) and each with clearance to build a cabin of up to 290 sqft (27 m²).

The cabin, constructed entirely in wood and plywood, enjoys a fairly isolated location and is privileged with its own source of water; a battery radio is the only device requiring an artificial source of energy. All interiors are clad in plywood painted white and some elements, such as the sliding door, are recycled from old buildings.

Rather than merely low-cost architecture, this is more about keeping things simple, easy and minimalist. Cheap-versus-expensive was not so much the organizing principle as was priority; and the priority here, as viewed by the architect, was that it should be playful, different and aesthetically pleasing. His aim was to combine common sense with the greater good of change and expression.

Although the cabin is small, there are many implied zones within each seemingly single space. The shape is simple, yet expressive. Its pure, unadorned architectural style makes it difficult to define what the cabin should or must be, thus enabling a constant redefining of the uses that it will take on throughout time.

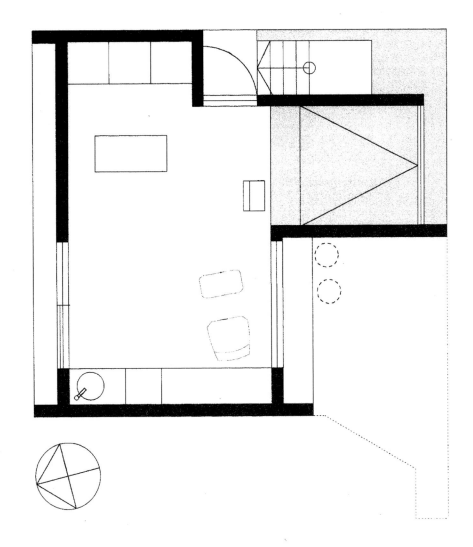

Although the cabin is small, there are many implied zones within each seemingly single space. The shape is simple, yet expressive. Its pure, unadorned architectural style makes it difficult to define what the cabin should or must be, thus enabling a constant re-defining of the uses that it will take on throughout time.

DRY Design
Lengau Lodge

Photographs: Undine Pröhl

Limpopo Province, South Africa

Lengau Lodge is located in the Limpopo Province in northern South Africa. The project program is a wildlife viewing lodge situated in the Welgevonden Game Reserve, a private wildlife preserve. Lengau Lodge consists of nine buildings occupying a total of 12,863 sqft (1195 m²).

Set on sloping land, the buildings are sited on existing level pads wherever possible to reduce the amount of grading. Shallow soil conditions allow for the footings to be doweled directly into bedrock. Eccentric local rock outcroppings are allowed to penetrate the concrete floors, creating plan anomalies in some of the buildings.

Three plan typologies have been utilized to respond to site conditions: the Wedge Plan, to accommodate perpendicular conjoining spaces so that the plans do not become too linear; Shear, in which linear plans shear and then rotate in relationship to each other to accommodate eccentricities in the topography, and to capture the best views; and Corner Links, with buildings joined at the corners, creating increased exterior surface area exposure.

The remote nature of the site requires that all sewage and water is dealt with on the site. Septic tanks overflow into anaerobic rock filters and then into two constructed wetlands. After additional processing through aerobic bio-filters the water that emerges from the constructed wetlands exceeds the minimal government standards for quality. The water from the wetlands is used either for irrigation purposes, or is fed into a watering hole for animals.

The buildings have brick and concrete bases with wooden roof timbers and thatched roofing. Modern space-making ideas are transcribed onto vernacular tradition to create buildings that use thick masonry walls on their south elevations, which house the infrastructure, while the north elevations use extensive glazing sheltered by concrete canopies to let in the low winter sun. A clerestory window level, which scoops natural light into the building, separates the masonry base from the wood roof timbers above.

The southern roof forms gentle hyperbolic parabaloid curves that take advantage of the plasticity of thatch, which is a highly effective insulating material. The concrete verandah roofs contain planters seeded with local short grasses. All bricks were locally manufactured and timber was obtained from sustainable sources. The doors and windows are made of sustainably harvested Australian hardwoods. The finished floors are in pigmented and polished concrete slabs heated with radiant heat tubing. There is no provision for air conditioning, as the high ceilings and large gable end windows allow effective cross-ventilation. These windows are screened by large shutters that cut light while allowing transmission of air.

Site plan

The project program is a wildlife viewing lodge situated in the Welgevonden Game Reserve. Lengau Lodge consists of nine buildings. Set on sloping land, the buildings are sited on existing level pads wherever possible to reduce the amount of grading.

Three plan typologies have been utilized to respond to site conditions: the Wedge Plan, to accommodate perpendicular conjoining spaces so that the plans do not become too linear; Shear, in which linear plans shear and then rotate in relationship to each other to accommodate eccentricities in the topography, and to capture the best views; and Corner Links, with buildings joined at the corners, creating increased exterior surface area exposure.

Central building - plan

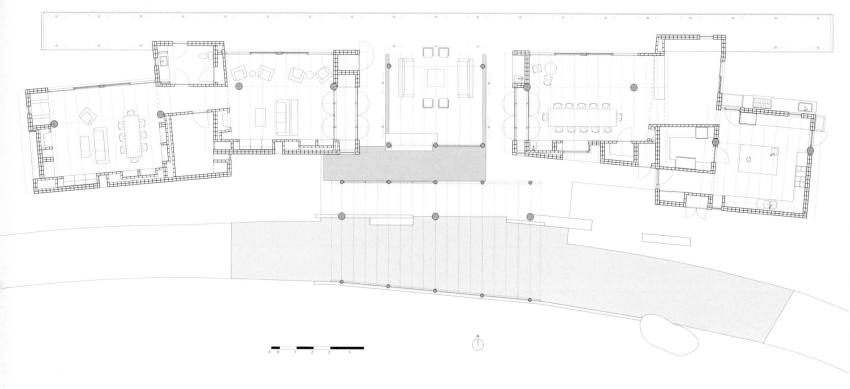

Central building - roof plan

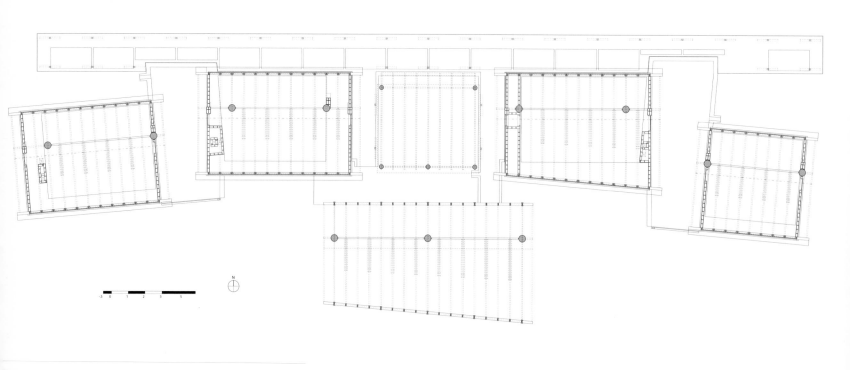

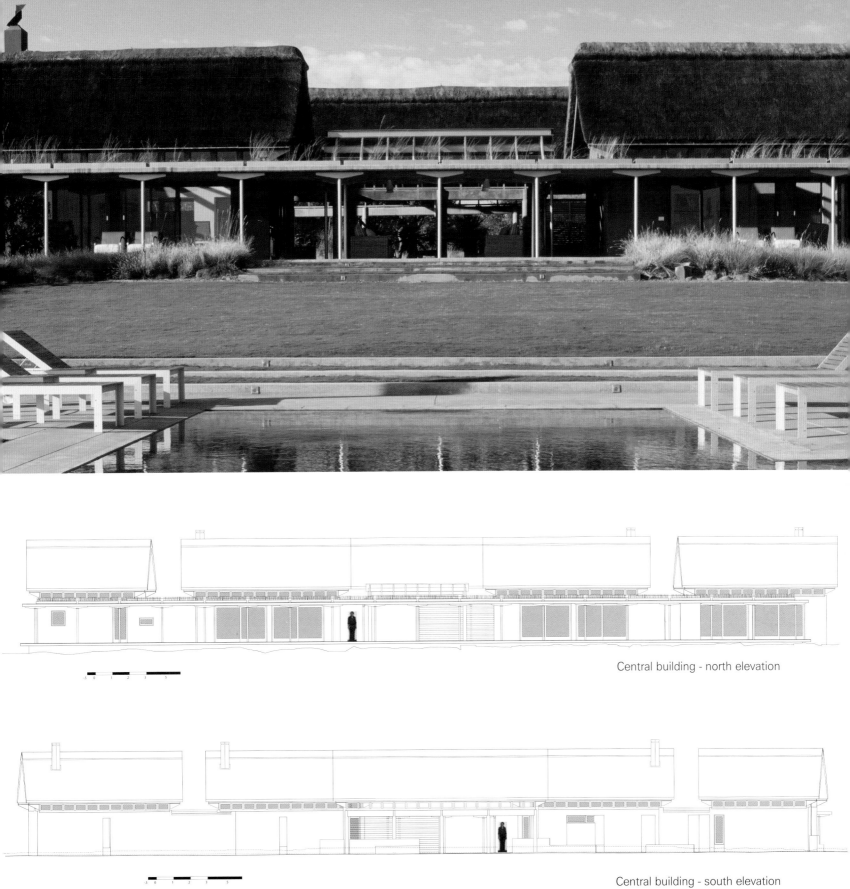

Central building - north elevation

Central building - south elevation

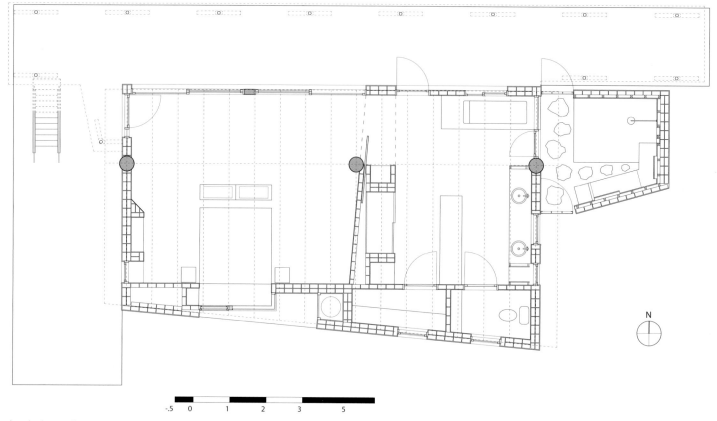

Sleeping lodge - plan

N

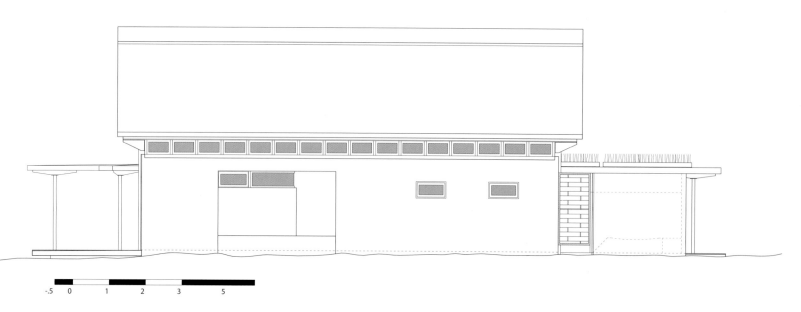

Sleeping lodge - South elevation

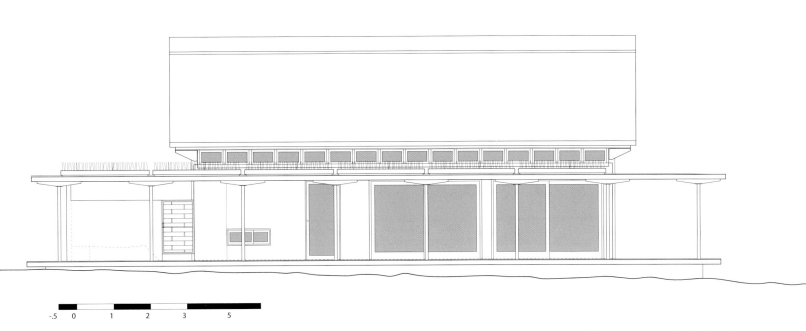

Sleeping lodge - North elevation

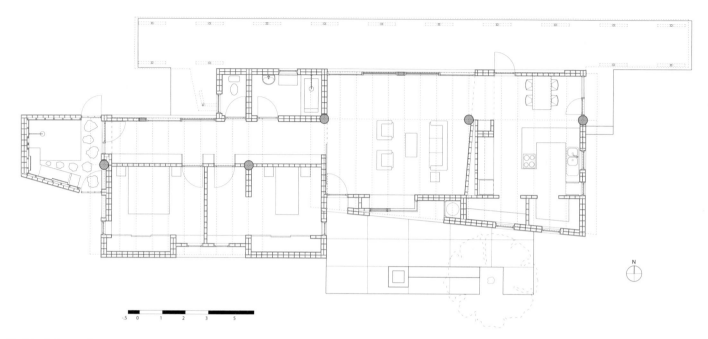

Staff building - plan

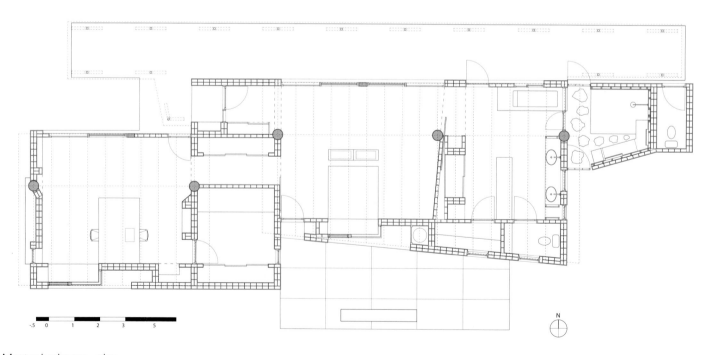

Master bedroom - plan

A clerestory window level, which scoops natural light into the building, separates the masonry base from the wood roof timbers above. There is no provision for air conditioning, as the high ceilings and large gable end windows allow effective cross-ventilation. These windows are screened by large shutters that cut light while allowing transmission of air.

Smiths Architects
Smith McLain Cabin

Photographs: Smiths Architects

Castle Rock, Colorado, USA

As a project the 186 sqft (17.3 m²) cabin represents two urban dwellers needs to escape the city. In a subdivided cattle ranch of 40 acre plots overlooking the Sangre De Cristo mountain range, the cabin is a modern day settlers claim. Perched on an outcropping of rocks at 9,800 feet it is an amalgam of the windblown Bristlecone pine and the tectonics of the early settlers cabins both indigenous to the area.

The cabin's skin alternately is tongue-and-groove cedar or 5/8" exterior plywood with 1x4 cedar slatting over 2x2 cedar battens. The design recalls the horizontal lines in the body of settlers cabins and the vertical quality of board and batten frequently used in the gable. Battens are installed directly behind 2x4 studs concealing plywood joints and linking vertically to roof joists. This configuration reveals the inner construction of studs spaced at 16" on center and as interrupted by king and trimmer studs at window and door openings. Programatically the screen allows for security shutters over windows and escape from the heat of mid-day sun.

The varying pitches and attenuated extensions of the roof form recall the Bristlecone as an expression of wind. Roof pitches respond to the program needs of awning at the entry and shelter/transition at the living area/ deck passage. The different heights set a heirarchy between the service (kitchen/ mud-room) side and the living area side. Galvanized corrugated metal roofing and details both inside and out assure longevity and link to the indigenous vocabulary of "ranch".

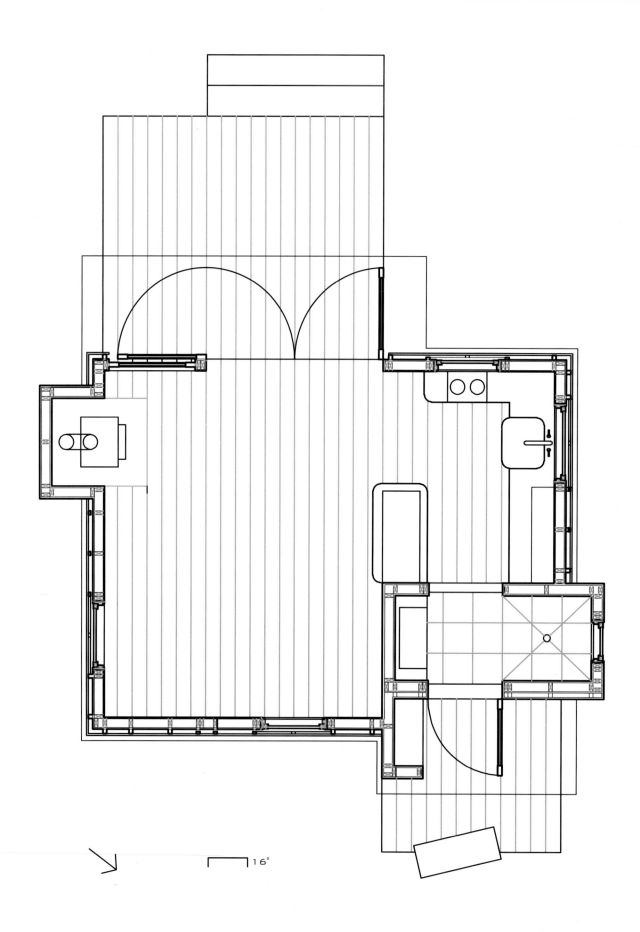

16"

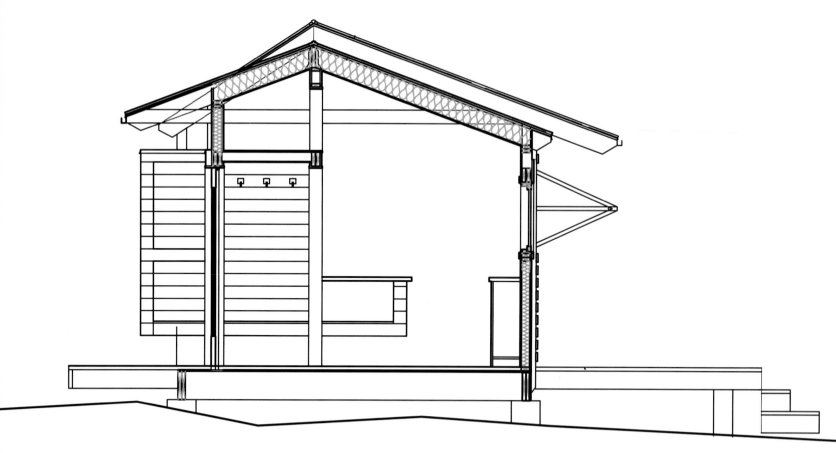

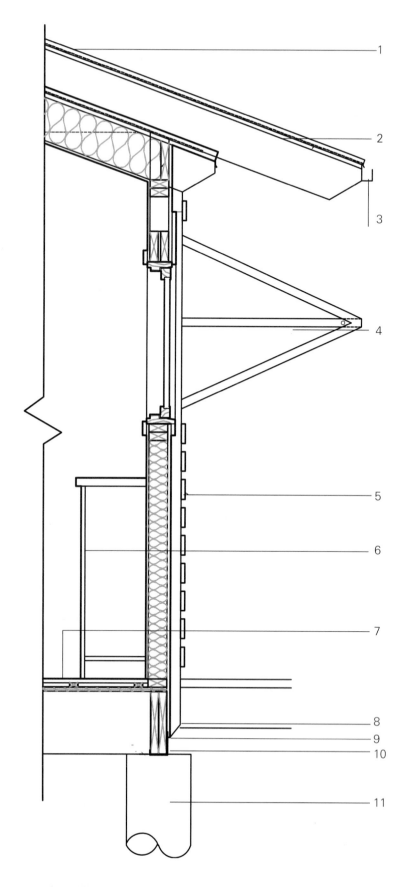

Wall Section

1. Corrugated metal roof (2´´ corrugations) on 30# felt on fl´´ plywood deck, R-30 insulation, plywood interior

2. Cedar boards in lieu of plywood at underside of exposed leaves

3. Custom 2-1/2´´x 2-1/2´´ galvanized gutter and drip edge

4. Steel shutter support

5. 1x4 cedar slating on 2x2 cedar battens on 5/8´´ exterior plywood (dark stain) 2x4 studs w/ R-13 batt insulation

6. Built-in cabinets of cedar boards and 2x4s, galvanized hinges and pulls

7. 3/4´´ x 6´´ character marked ash wood floor on 1x2 sleepers

8. 45⁰ cut at base of battens corresponds to b.o. plywood

9. Bottom of plywood

10. Galvanized metal base wrap

11. Concrete pier

Lundberg Design
Breuer/Lundberg Cabin

Photographs: JD Peterson

Sonoma, California, USA

The cabin sits in the middle of 12 acres (4.8 Ht) of redwood trees, overlooking a wooded river canyon to the northeast, and is about 2 hours drive north from San Francisco. It is a magical place where I go almost every weekend to recharge. It is modest in scale, only 1100 sqft (102 m²), but the large deck and open plan make it feel spacious. Other elements on the property are a platform "safari" tent for guests, a 3000 sqft (278 m²) fenced vegetable garden, and the start of a greenhouse/office structure.

Most of the project has been built using re-claimed materials from various projects over the years. The windows are all steel sash from at last count 5 different remodel projects. The pool is perhaps the most notable example – it used to be a water tank for livestock. At 25 feet (7.5 m) diameter and 14 feet (4.25 m) deep it provides a wonderful "black hole" of water, particularly in a full moon.

It is a cook's kitchen, with an 8 foot by 8 foot (2.40 m) island then tends to become the center of activity during meal preparation. The floors are a multicolored slate, which is the only material that does not show everything that the dogs tend to drag in. The exterior siding is reclaimed redwood. Eventually the interior walls will be thin strips of Montana white pine, but right now they are sheathing plywood. The bed cantilevers out over the loft edge to provide a little more room upstairs, and would not be good for someone with vertigo.

Some elements are custom designed for the cabin, such as the firewood holder. But many of the pieces are rejects from other projects, like the coffee table that was designed for the Diva Hotel (it has a flaw in the casting). The entire project has been built by the office or myself over the years (big food parties tend to help), and continues to serve as a source of education and inspiration for the entire office.

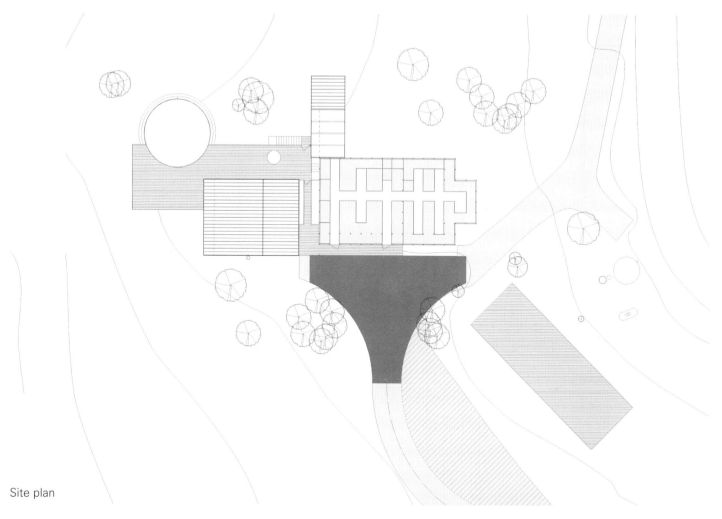

Site plan

Basement plan

1. Basement
2. Crawl space

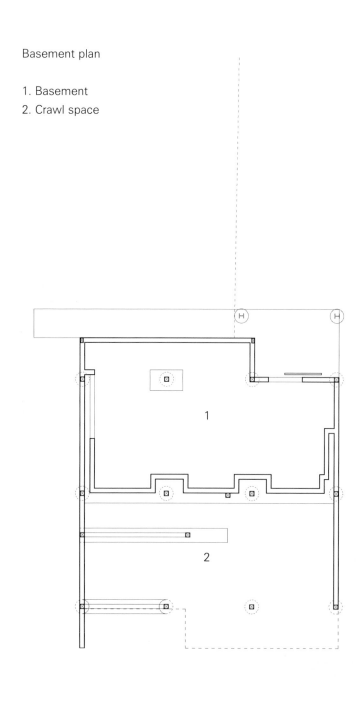

Ground floor plan

1. Living
2. Dining
3. Storage
4. Bath
5. Closet
6. Kitchen

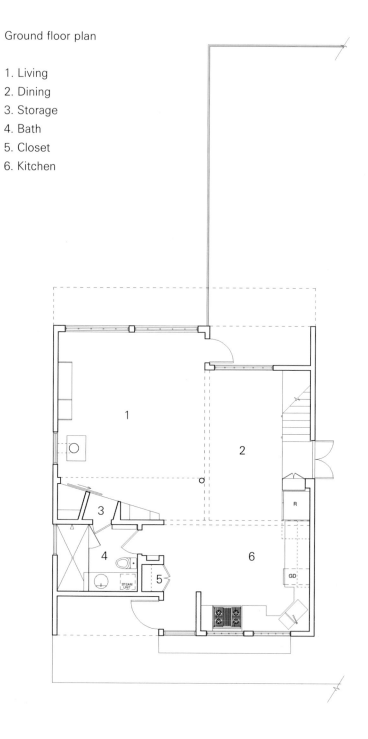

Mezzanine plan

1. Bedroom

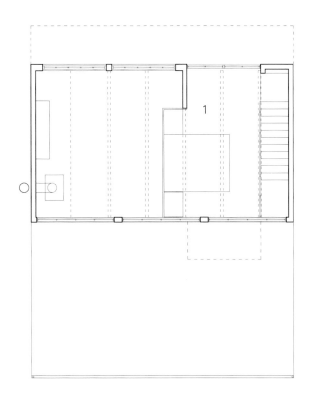

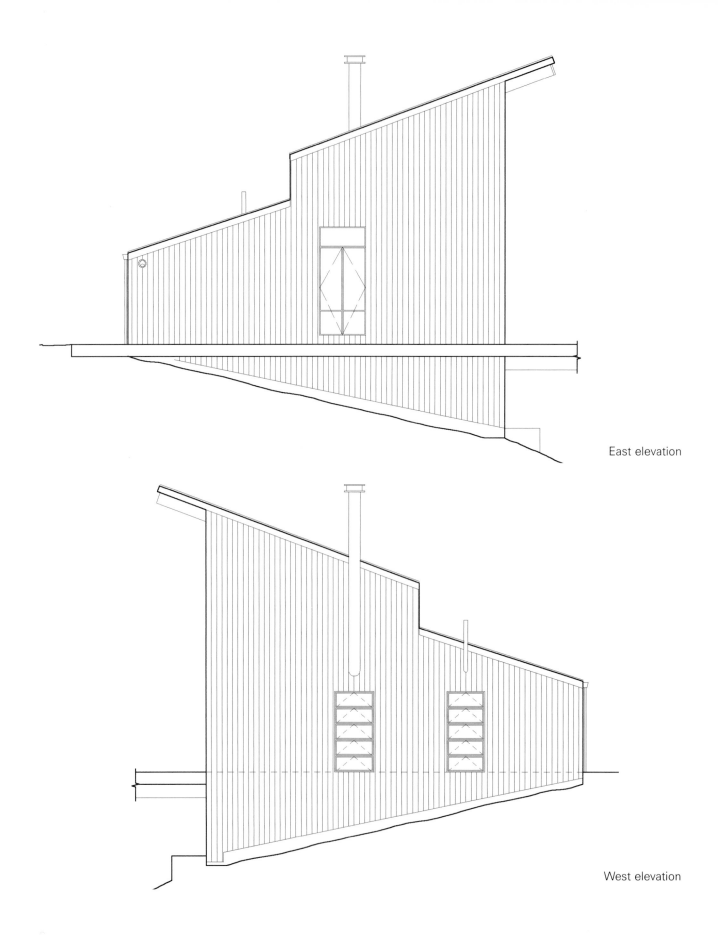

East elevation

West elevation

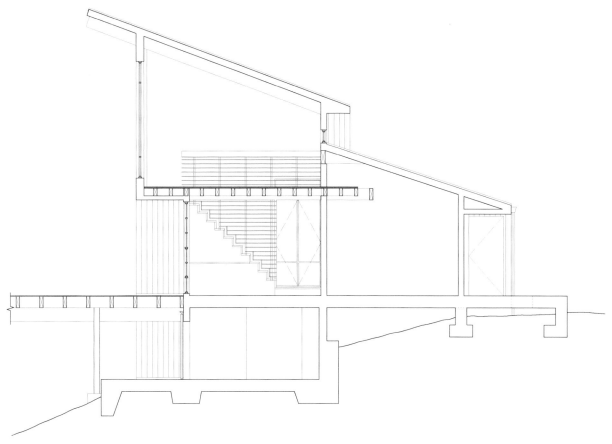

South elevation

North elevation

Rolf Åsberg
House Boat

Photographs: James Silverman

Gothenbourg, Sweden

From the drawing board, it took only a year to get this floating house built and towed to its current residence in Gothenburg's harbor. The houseboat itself rests on two six-meter-long pontoons, one with fresh water and the other with a holding-tank. The houseboat itself has all the modern conveniences, a shower, toilet, sauna and the kitchen with a gas stove, fridge, freezer and fan.

The first impression is of space and light. Large windows and sliding glass doors let the light in, with panoramic views over the sea from most angles.

The goal was to get a modern, light and simple boat, primarily achieved through the use of aluminum, birch and light materials. The colors that were selected for the interior were white and dark navy blue to match the nature that surrounds the little home.

Simplicity is essential in compact living, and the secret of the houseboat is how the space is designed. In this program, compact living has become a beautiful art form. The result is that the kitchen is combined with all the areas: the dining section, bathroom, living room, office (which is also a bedroom), sauna, fireplace and sleeping compartments. Many of the spaces have double functions. Another key that gives the interior a feeling of space and harmony is efficient storage. The benches in the kitchen provide this with large spaces underneath. The living room has a table with boxes to put things in and in the combined office/guestroom you can put the table up against the wall and pull out a bed.

A firewood stove faces the living room, although the sauna also provides some heating. The home has a 200V electrical system which also uses a built-in 12 volt solar energy system.

Inside, the walls are clad in birch-plywood and outside in a material called "Formaica". The insulation is extruded foam.

The only thing missing is the transportation of the boat, which requires a towboat. Fortunately, this is only done twice a year: once in the summertime, to a more peaceful location, and then back to the city in the autumn.

The living room enjoys magnificent views through large windows equipped with simple white curtains for when the sun is too bright. The rest of the furniture is made of beech and oak for a warm, natural feel.

The kitchen has been placed at one of the corners for the most efficient use possible. An oak ladder leads to the sleeping compartments, behind which is the sauna. The fireplace serves

dual functions, both for the living room and the sauna. It includes a sliding door of metal that you can pull down to lead the heat backwards to the sauna or pull up to use as a fireplace.

Todd Saunders & Tommie Wilhelmsen
Finland Project

Photographs: contributed by Saunders & Wilhelmsen Arkitektur AB

Aaland, Finland

The client wished to have a small, compact house, yet one that would meet a number of specific requirements. The constraints of the site, combined with budget restrictions, dictated the size of the house, which measures 452 sqft (42 m^2) in area. In retrospect, however, the architects concede that the project was made much more interesting with the ever-present question of how to make a small building feel large.

The building has been conceived as a long continuous timber structure - a folded space that you move along and through, over and under. It is an architectural landscape comprising all the elements of the house: walls, floor, roof, and terrace. Rooms can be either separated by sliding glass doors or melded as a single space when the doors are open. Or, for example, the open-air space between the kitchen and bedroom can be incorporated into the living spaces, creating one large, fluid indoor/outdoor room.

Views from the interior are of the surrounding pine forest, while the many islands around Aland can be fully appreciated from the roof terrace.

One of the most striking aspects of this house is that every square inch of space has been utilized. There is absolutely no wasted space, and the space that is created often has two- or three-fold functions. Considering hallways mostly a waste of space, the designers decided to leave such distributing elements out. There is ample seating room on the roof for social gatherings, or intimate dinners, while the "all room" between the kitchen and bedroom can have as many uses as the inhabitants see fit. As envisioned by the designers, this is a house without borders, one that can never be compact in the negative sense of the word.

Another unique aspect of the house is that it is environmentally responsible. It is insulated with woven linseed fibers and all the wood is protected with cold-pressed linseed oil. All materials are from a local sawmill; and the house itself is built on pillars so that the roots of the surrounding trees were left 100% untouched by the construction process.

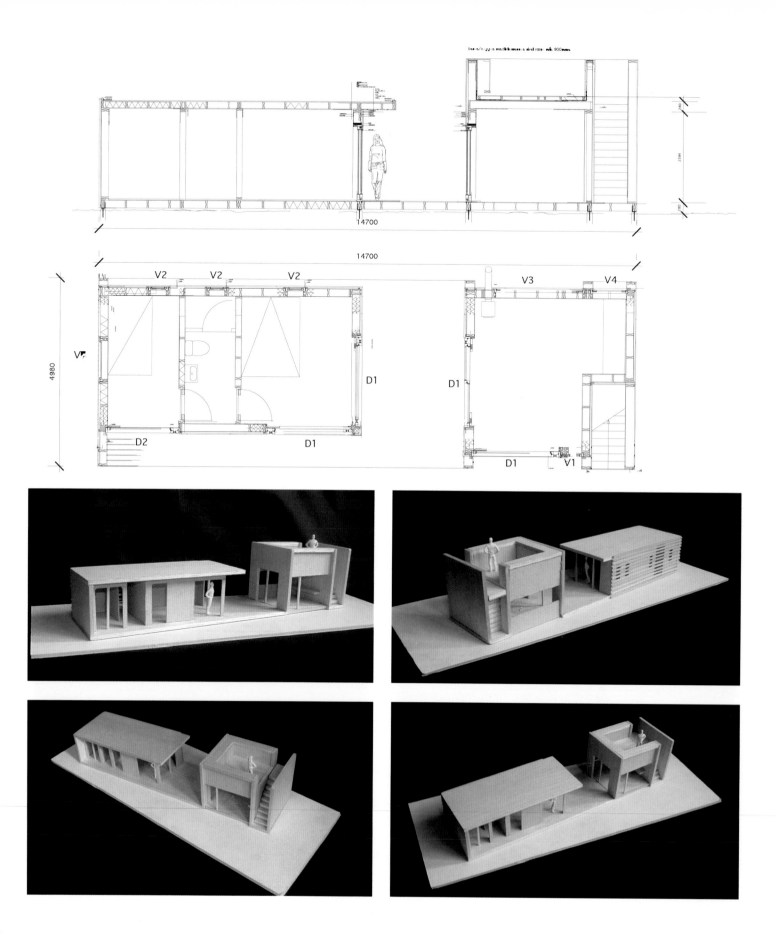

The client wished to have a small, compact house, yet one that would meet a number of specific requirements. The constraints of the site, combined with budget restrictions, dictated the size of the house, which measures 42 m² in area.

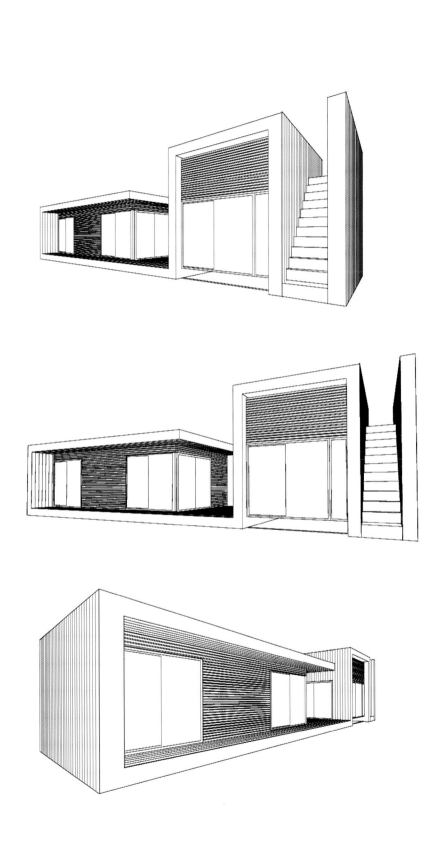

Taylor Smyth Architects
Sunset Cabin

Photographs: Ben Rahn / A-Frame Inc. & Taylor Smyth

Lake Simcoe, Canada

Since the clients entertain up to 15 overnight visitors at a time during the summer at their family cottage on Lake Simcoe, their personal privacy is a prime concern, for which they requested a separate sleeping cabin for their personal use. Their primary requirement was to be able to lie in bed and watch the sunset.

The project consists of a single 275 sqft (25.5m²) room. All components are built in, including the bed and a wall of storage cabinets on either side. The floor of the cabin extends outside towards the lake to become a deck with access to an outdoor shower enclosed by a cedar screen.

The cabin is fabricated of clear cedar for window frames, doors and cladding. The cedar is untreated, gradually turning silver and blending the structure into the landscape. All interior surfaces are birch veneer plywood panels - floors, back wall and ceiling and storage, so no re-painting is required.

The cabin was first constructed in a parking lot in Toronto over a period of 4 weeks by a group of craftsmen who usually build furniture. This allowed for details to be worked out precisely and all the components to be pre-fabricated. These were numbered, disassembled and reconstructed on site in just 10 days. Prefabrication reduced costs by an estimated 30% by decreasing construction time and simplifying the difficulties of working at a remote, sloping site, and hence reduced labor costs.

Three walls of the cabin are floor to ceiling glass, wrapped by an exterior horizontal cedar screen on two sides for privacy and sun shading. A large cut-out in the screen is carefully located to provide spectacular views of the setting sun from the bed. Gaps between the individual members of the screen increase arbitrarily as the cabin gets closer to the lake, framing snapshots of random, seemingly abstract compositions of vegetation, lake and sky. The clients had potentially conflicting requirements for maximum views and openness, yet combined with privacy from the main cottage. The density of the screen gradually diminishes as it moves away from the main cottage. The screen obscures views in, while enabling views out.

Practical requirements dictated configuration in the case of the long glass wall that angles away from the outer cedar screen to allow space to wash the windows. The result is a fascinating play of light on the glass.

The cabin is located on an existing level piece of ground, chosen both for its views and to avoid the need to remove any trees. It is supported on 2 steel beams resting on 4 concrete caissons. This allows the cabin to rest lightly on the site, with minimal disruption to vegetation.

A Green Roof, planted with sedums and herbs, allows the cabin to blend into the landscape due to the visibility of the roof from the main cottage at the top of the hill. Passive Energy Saving Measures have also been incorporated: the exterior cedar screen provides sun shading, while doors at each end capitalize on lake breezes and provide cross ventilation.

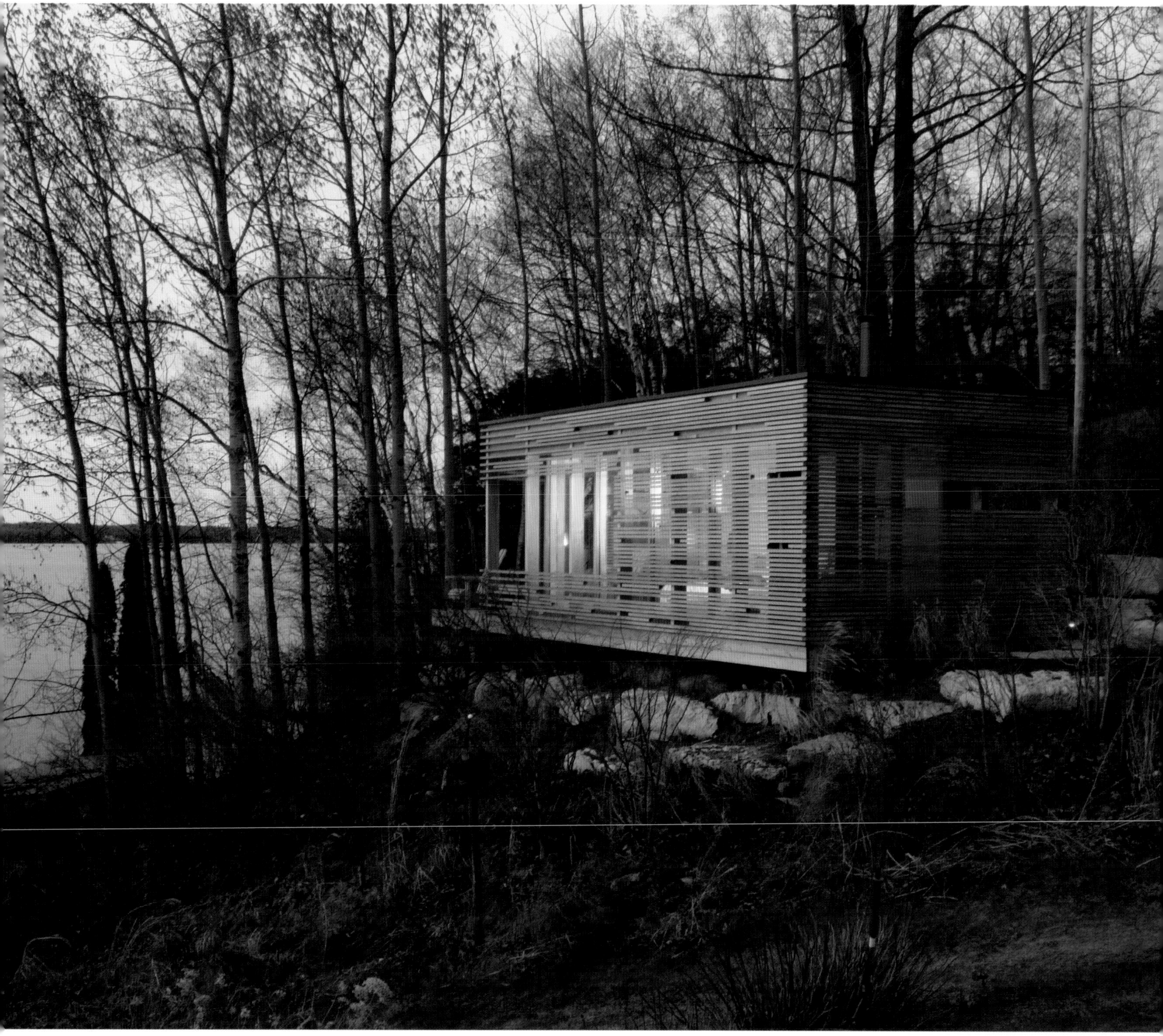

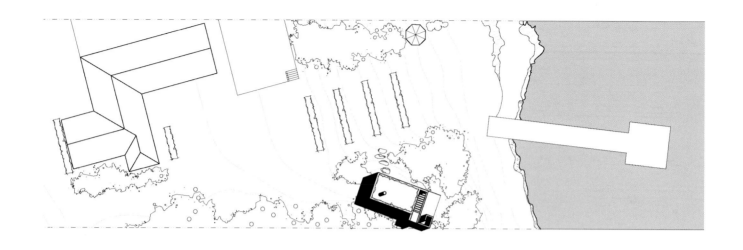

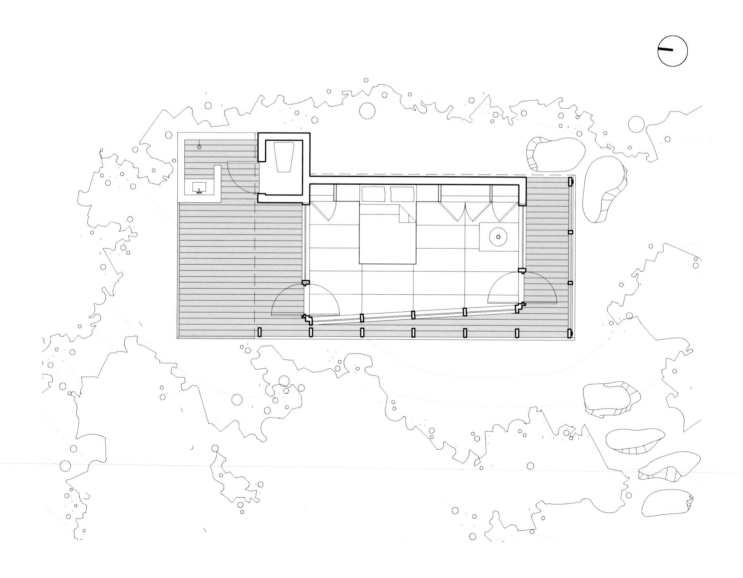

The cabin is located on an existing level piece of ground, chosen both for its views and to avoid the need to remove any trees. It is supported on 2 steel beams resting on 4 concrete caissons. This allows the cabin to rest lightly on the site, with minimal disruption to vegetation.

© Taylor Smyth

© Ben Rahn / A-Frame Inc.

© Ben Rahn / A-Frame Inc.

119

© Taylor Smyth

© Ben Rahn / A-Frame Inc.

© Ben Rahn / A-Frame Inc.

© Taylor Smyth

Practical requirements dictated configuration in the case of the long glass wall that angles away from the outer cedar screen to allow space to wash the windows. The result is a fascinating play of light on the glass.

Vandeventer + Carlander Architects

Camano Island Cabin

Photographs: Steve Keating

Camano Island, WA, USA

This 352 sqft (32.38 m²) cabin is located on a high windswept bluff above the sea with views across Saratoga Passage to Whidbey Island and the Olympic Mountains. Located on a flat bench midway between the uphill access road and the bluff, the cabin sits below adjoining uphill neighbors, thus bringing about the need for a sense of privacy to be incorporated into the design. Utilizing an existing concrete foundation and adjoining garden, the solution mediates between this need for privacy from the neighbors, while at the same time promoting a connection - however minimum - to the garden and views.

The solution, a basic wood-frame box with two large pairs of doors that open both to the garden and views, nonetheless creates a somewhat introverted home shielded from the strong gales that often sweep up from the sea. A secondary element, a metal clad wall, was used as a privacy screen that also incorporates the garden.

A "plane" in the form of a simple shed-like roof was inserted to create a sleeping loft. The void between the box and plane was glazed to reinforce the formal composition while affording views and light.

Construction was kept basic as it was the owners themselves who acted as their own general contractors and finishing carpenters.

The main box is wood framed and clad in Fiber cement panels, while the secondary elements were clad in metal panels for weather resistance and durability. Windows and doors were aluminum storefront-style, thus reinforcing the low maintenance requirements. A stained concrete slab was used for the main floor.

The owners finished the cabin using cherry and maple plywood fashioned in the same formal vocabulary and construction techniques exhibited on the exterior. Heat is provided by a Rais wood stove and augmented by electric coils buried in the concrete slab.

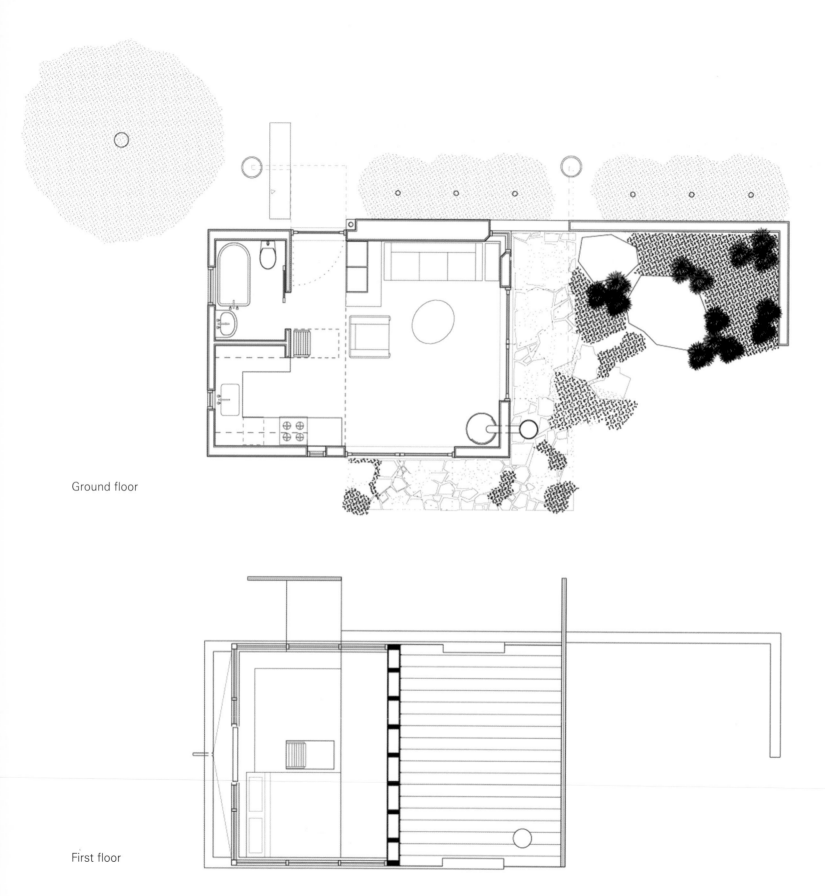

Ground floor

First floor

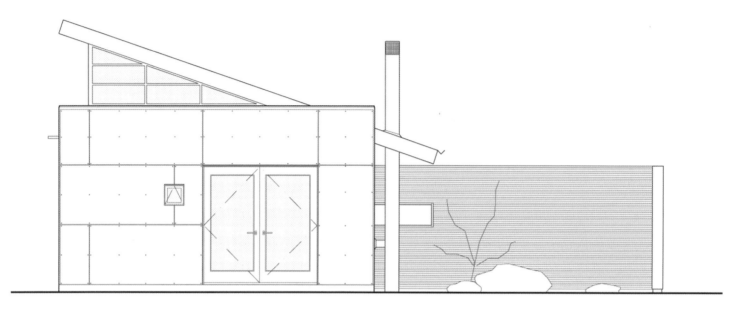

West elevation

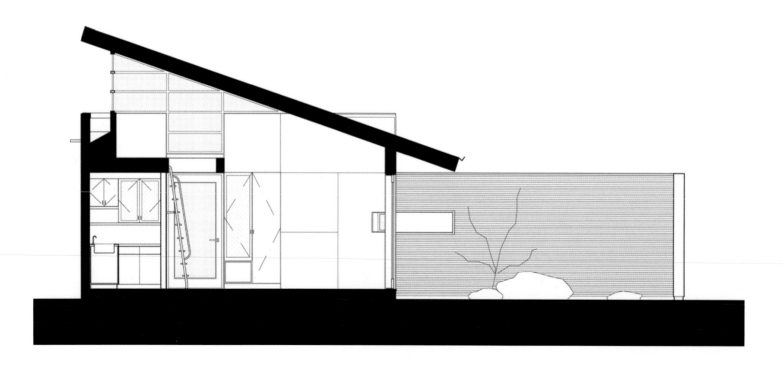

North elevation

South elevation

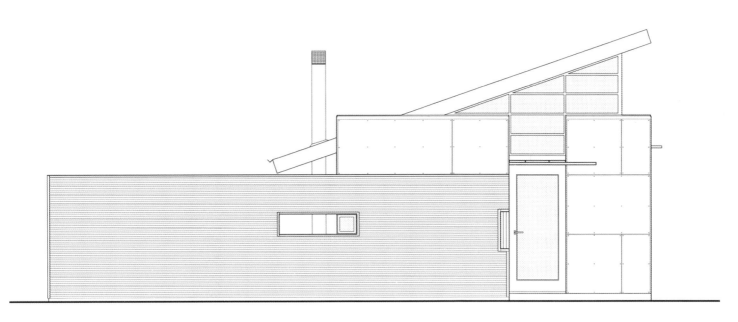

East elevation

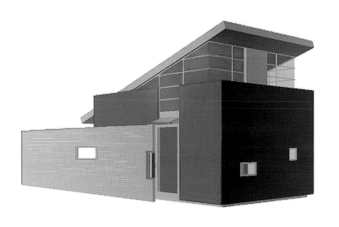

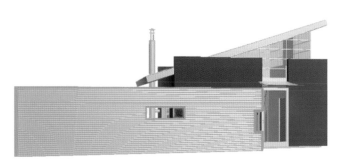

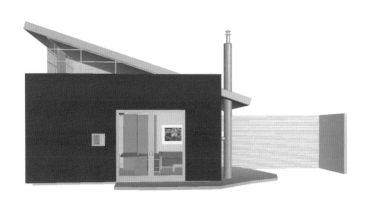

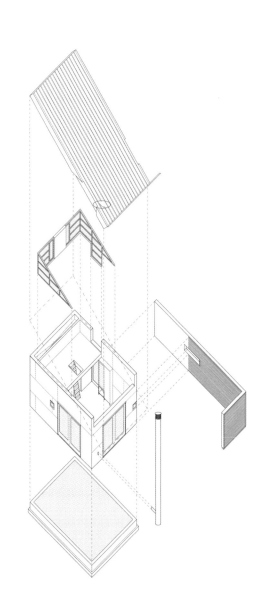

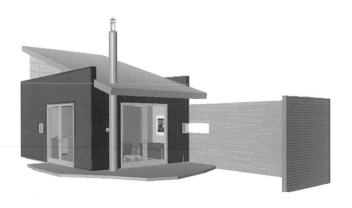

The owners finished the cabin using cherry and maple plywood fashioned in the same formal vocabulary and construction techniques exhibited on the exterior. Heat is provided by a Rais wood stove and augmented by electric coils buried in the concrete slab.

L-Architectes
Maison Perret

Photographs Jean-Michel Landecy

Cully, Canton Vaud, Switzerland

The house is perched in a vertiginous setting on the boundary between forests and vineyards in the Lavaux conservation area, which is soon to be registered as a UNESCO protected site, above Lake Leman.

Commissioned by the freeride skier Dominique Perret, the house has been designed to take advantage of its steep setting. It seems to sit precariously on the slope, as if it might tip forward and slide down the hill at any moment; however, its foundations have been well dug into the slope of the mountain, so much so that the first-floor back room is almost entirely underground. Furthermore, in choice of materials, construction logic and architectural style, it constantly alludes to, and draws on for inspiration, traditional high-altitude mountain huts.

The sweeping landscape is drawn into the interior of the house through south-facing floor to ceiling glazing that completely disappears, via sunken tracks, when open. A cozier ambience has been achieved through the application of an opposite strategy in the depths of the house, where a slope-facing space has been sunken into the ground and is centered on a fireplace.

Every square inch of the interior is a skillful demonstration of space-saving strategies. Niches fill the space beneath the wooden staircase and freestanding kitchen units serve to divide the space between the kitchen and living room.

With a total surface area of 1400 sqft (130 m²), the volume of the house is 18010 cft (510 m³). The steep slope and the unpaved access road severely limited the possibilities for in-situ construction. The entire house was therefore prefabricated off site, with the exception of the natural larch planking that cloaks the entire building, from the spacious terrace, to all exterior walls, where they have been placed sideways in front of certain windows to allow just enough space for views, and culminating in the roof.

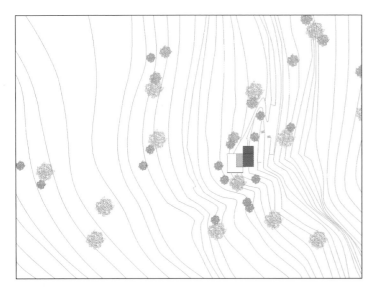

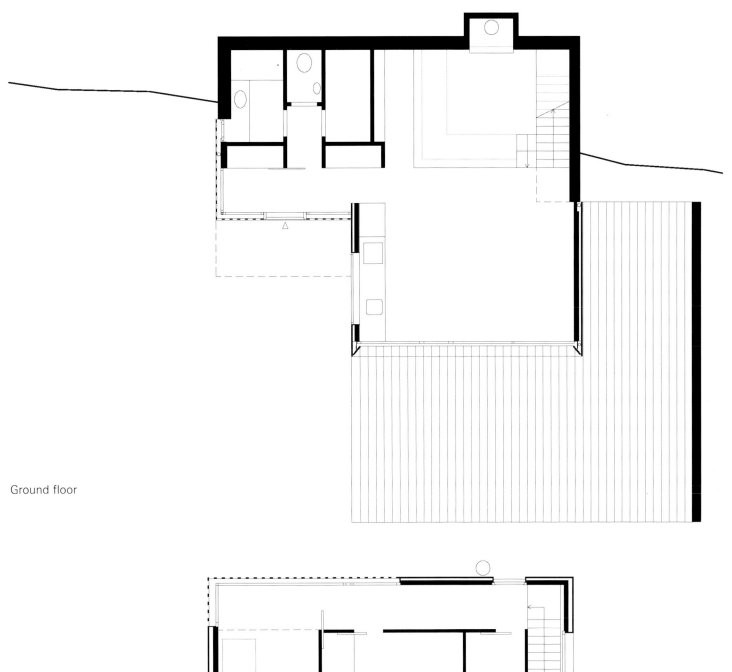

Ground floor

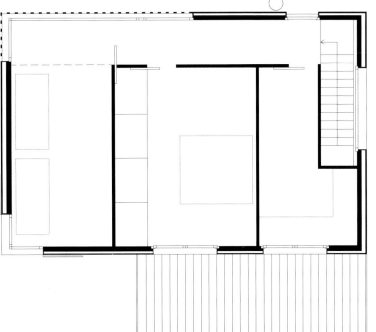

First floor

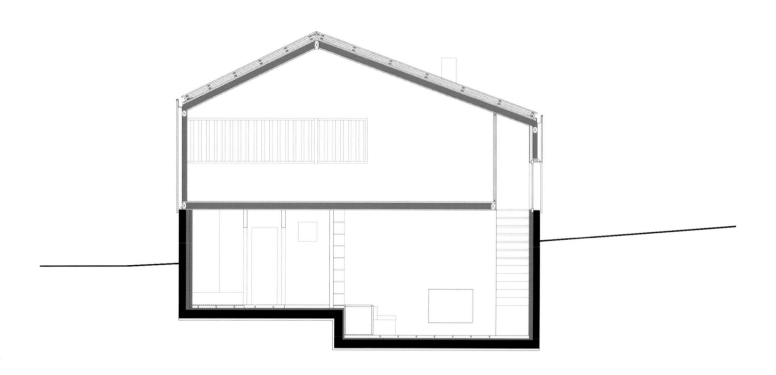

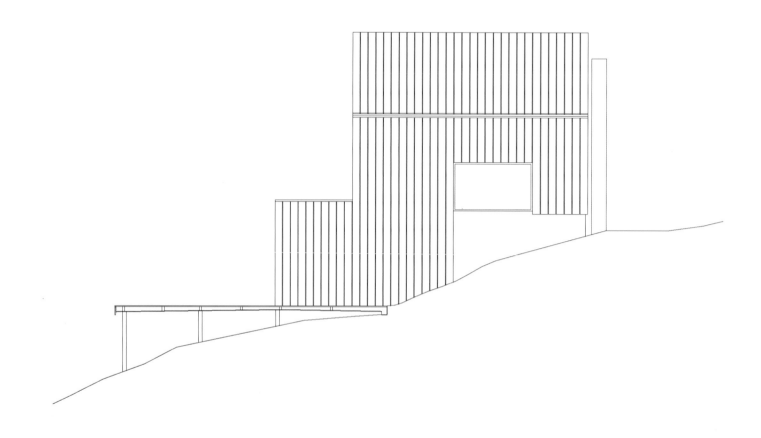

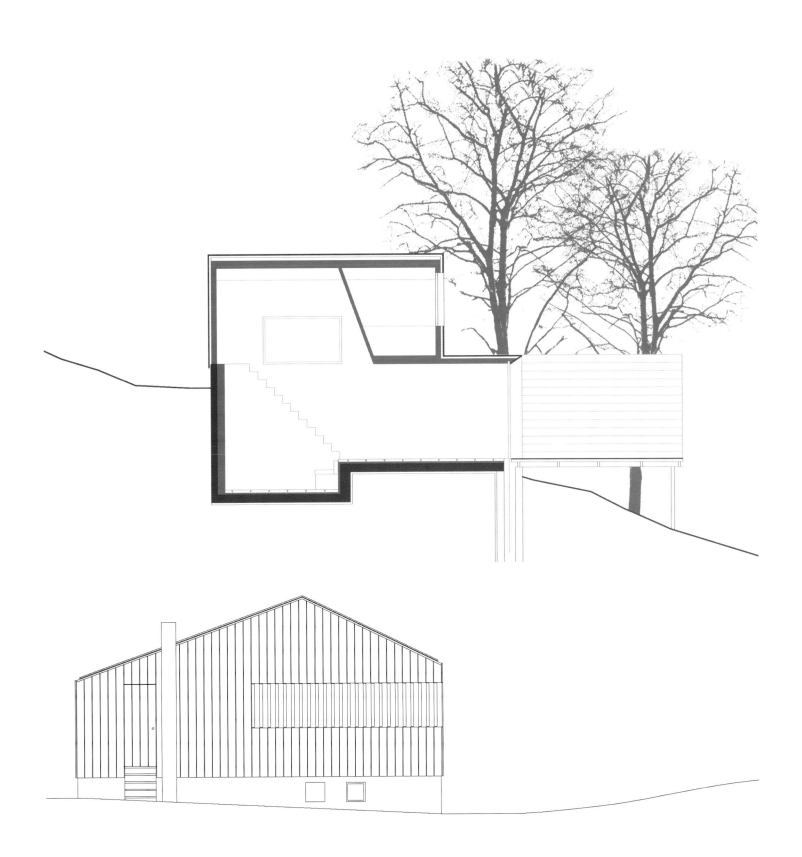

The sweeping landscape is drawn into the interior of the house through south-facing floor to ceiling glazing. A cozier ambience has been achieved through the application of an opposite strategy in the depths of the house, where a slope-facing space has been sunken into the ground and is centered on a fireplace. Every square inch of the interior is a skillful demonstration of space-saving strategies. Niches fill the space beneath the wooden staircase and freestanding kitchen units serve to divide the space between the kitchen and living room.

Strindberg Arkitekter AB
The Red House

Photographs: Gudrun Thielemann

Drag, Kalmar, Sweden

This little red summerhouse at Drag is beautifully situated to the north of Kalmar and Kalmar Sound. The client wanted a commanding character for this project, which is a partial remodeling and partially new construction.

Structures commonly seen in the Swedish countryside such as cabins, farmhouse and even gardening sheds served as inspiration for the program. The architect wished to achieve a simple overall shape, with sculptural volumes and reduced detailing. The façade was painted in the Swedish tradition, using red paint from the town of Falun where the pigment is a bi-product from the old copper mine.

The first phase of the project consisted of work on "the father's house", followed by the task of transforming a common Swedish summerhouse dating from the 1940s into an interpretation of the Swedish "red Stuga".

The "father's house" is a study as well as a retreat for the father when his grown kids come to visit. Its design was inspired by the idea of a simple garden shed, however here with open views and an overhanging roof to shade the windows; in fact, this is the only volume in the project with projecting eaves. Because of its proximity to the sea, it has been raised above the ground and rests on poles.

The "new" house makes use of fragments of walls from the former house as well as the shape of its foundation; otherwise, nothing is as it was before. Two similar volumes facing in different directions stand close to each other and are linked by a small entrance. One of them is an open-plan body to be used as living room and kitchen, the other has been divided for bedrooms and has a small loft above.

The strict volumes are softened by light and shadow, due to the depth and close placing of the wooden cladding and the matte red paint that tends to absorb light.

The houses were nominated for the Swedish red paint prize of 2004 (Rödfärgspriset 2004).

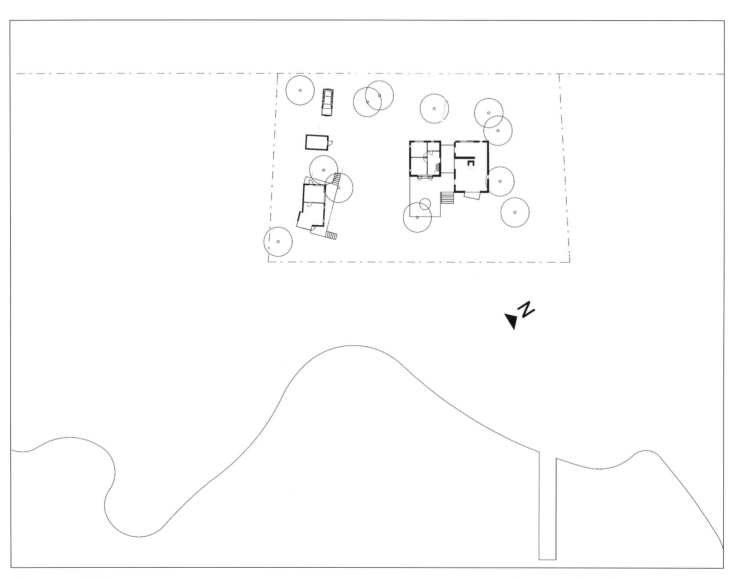

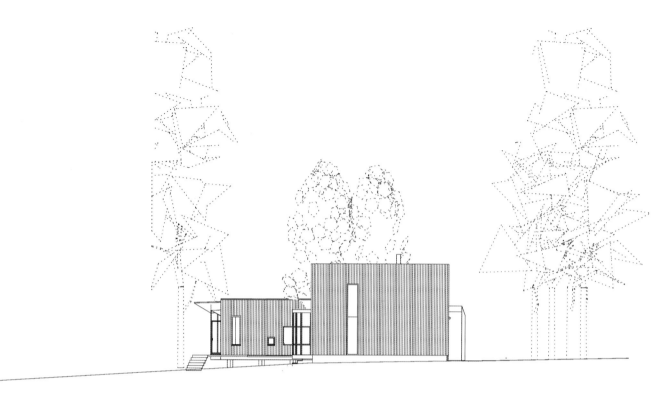

Northeast elevation

Elevation facing the sea

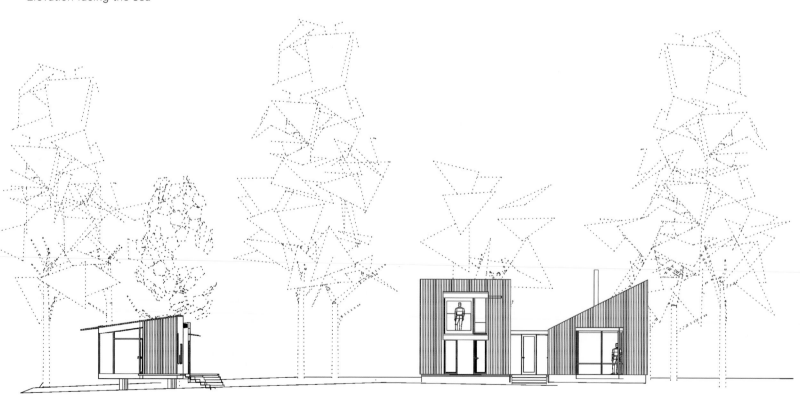

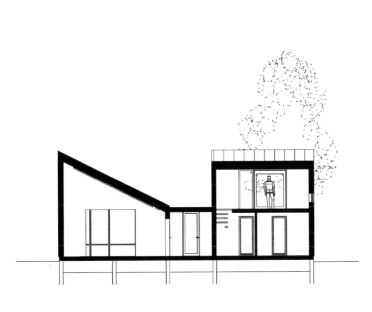

Jarmund / Vigsnæs

Cabin Nordmarka

Photographs: Nils Petter Dale

Located in a clearing in a thick forest, this cozy, light-filled cabin does not respond to its immediate surroundings; rather, it has been designed with views of the rolling hills and lakes dotting the horizon toward the south in mind.

Not only are choice views guaranteed in this way, but also as much natural light as possible - such an important aspect in this far northern region. This has also been achieved by splitting the angle of the extensively glazed main façade: the larger end of the angle is tipped slightly toward the southwest, its massive window catching light throughout the day, and particularly the final rays of the sunset. The shorter end of the façade's angle, on the other hand, is directed ever so slightly toward the southeast, flooding the cabin with morning sun.

Having taken such care to ensure the absolute maximum amount of available natural light, the logical next step was to create an interior layout that would effectively distribute it. The solution is a floor plan gathered around a double-height internal central space, which works in a way as a minor urban piazza of the building. Additional light is brought in along the ridge of the roof in the form of ample skylights.

The house, sitting on 1292 sqft (120 m²) of floor area, has been well equipped with spaces both for privacy and for social living. The size scale of the spaces go from the small cave-like children's bedrooms to the soaring volume of the living room, around which daily activity evolves.

Although the final look of the house is clearly anything but "traditional", its use of materials certainly has drawn on the logic and centuries' old wisdom of Norwegian cabin-building: a black-stained wooden shell to absorb sunlight, with a luminous interior entirely clad in light-toned, unstained wood to amplify the sense of light.

Ground floor

1. Entrance
2. Bathroom
3. Ski prepare
4. Food storage
5. Kitchen
6. Living
7. Main bedroom
8. Bedroom
9. Terrace

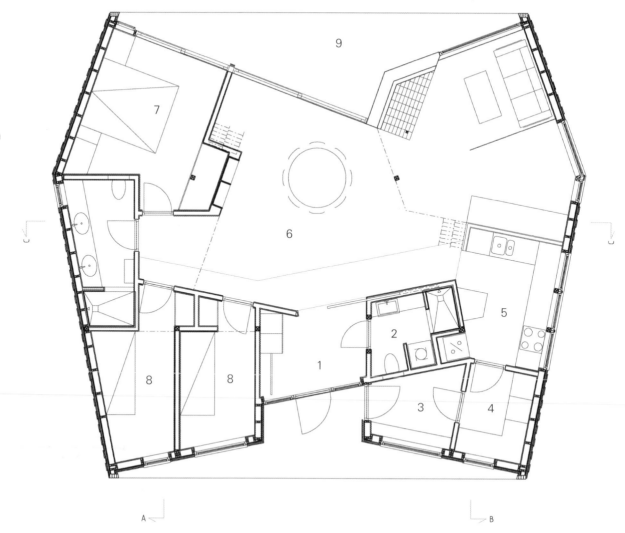

First floor

1. Bedroom
2. TV room
3. Technical room

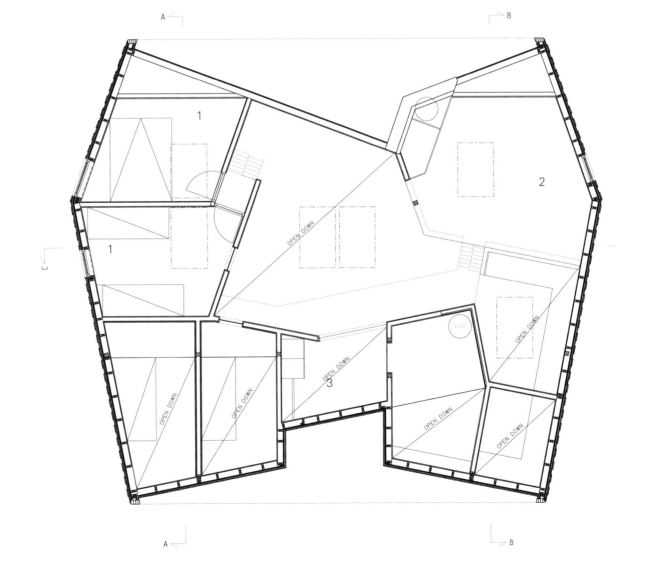

West elevation

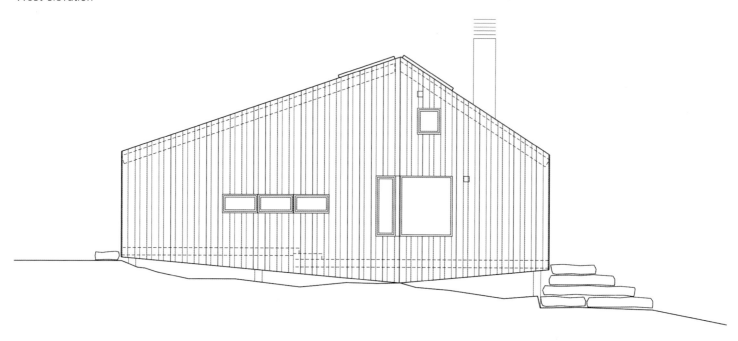

North elevation

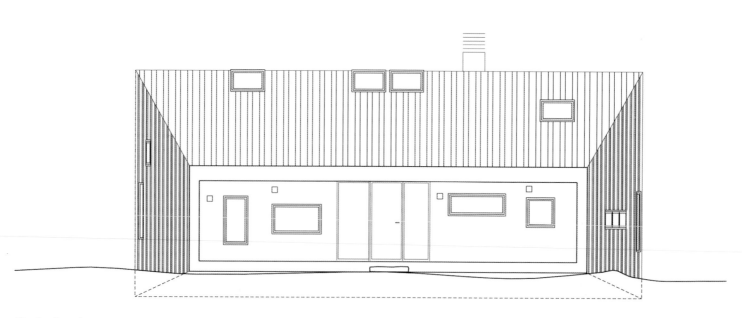

East elevation

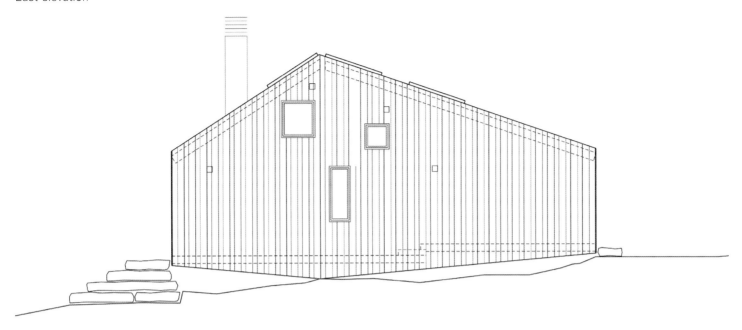

South elevation

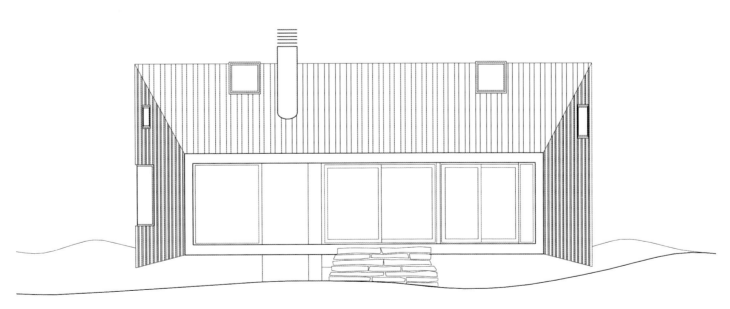

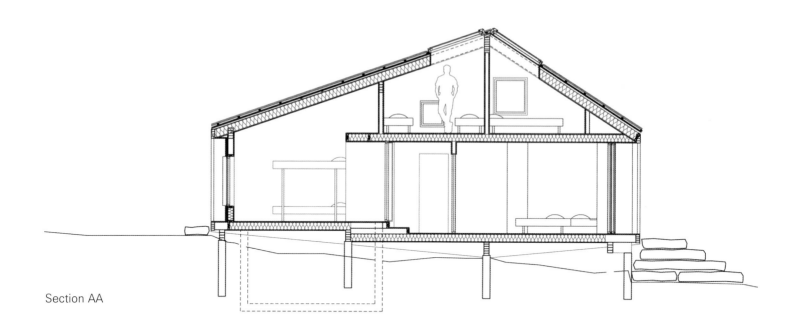

Section AA

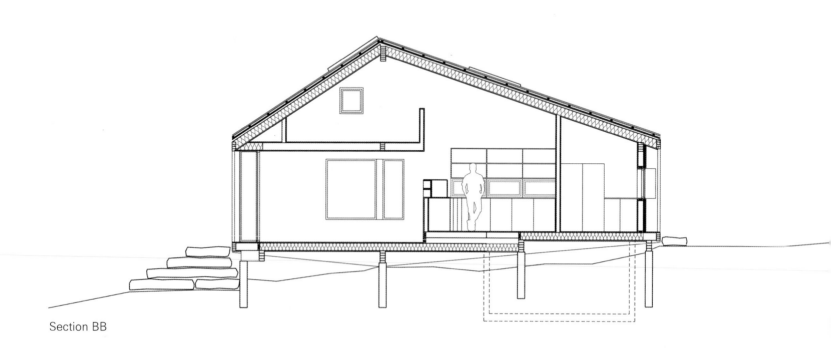

Section BB

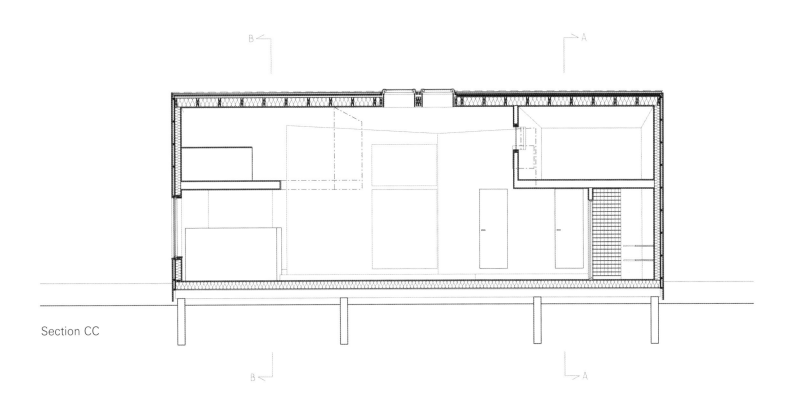

Section CC

The house, sitting on 120 square meters of floor area, has been well equipped with spaces both for privacy and for social living. The size scale of the spaces go from the small cave-like children's bedrooms to the soaring volume of the living room, around which daily activity evolves.

24H-architecture

Extension to House on Övre Gla

Photographs: Christian Richters

Övre Gla, Sweden

This project sets out to provide extra space to an original wood cabin from the 1800's located on the shore of Lake Övre Gla, in the nature reserve of Glaskogen, in Sweden. According to Swedish building regulations it is not allowed to make an extension that exceeds the maximum floor area. A second priority for the building regulations is its proximity to the border of the property, in this case the extraordinary location along a stream which forms part of the site boundary.

To make maximum use of the possibilities given by the building regulations, the extension that 24 h made to the existing cabin was designed to evolve; the building can literally adjust itself to its environment depending on weather conditions, the season or the number of occupants. The extension unfurls like a butterfly; during the winter it's a cocoon, compact, with a double skin against the cold. During the summer the building can change its form or, like a butterfly, unfold its wings for extra shelter during rainy days.

When the space is at its biggest, the senses are aroused to the max: living above the rushing waters of the stream.

The organic shape of the house blends naturally into the environment of the woodland. Traditional roofing materials (Stickor), that were common in Sweden many years ago, have been maintained. In due time the wood surfaces will bleach to acquire a silvery-grey appearance, blending smoothly into the wild and rocky environment of the forest.

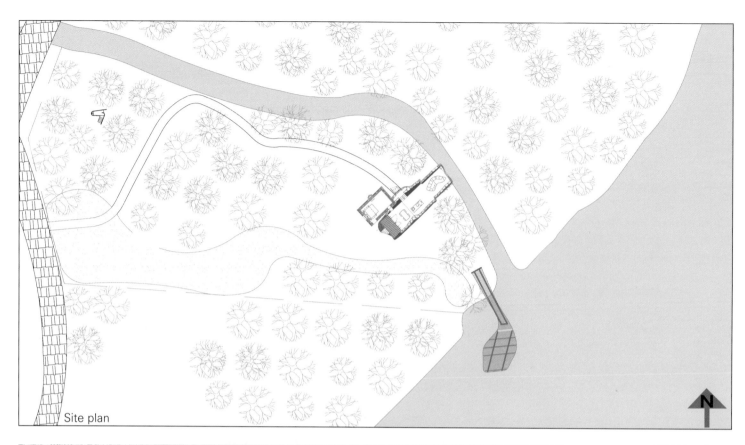

Site plan

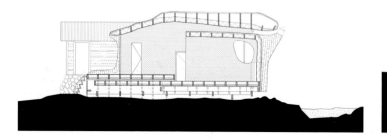
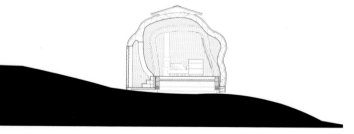

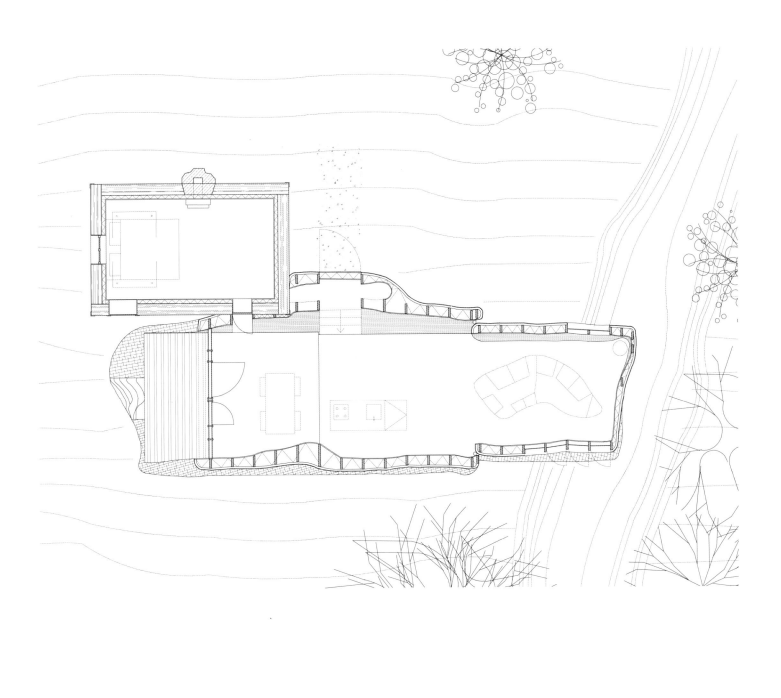

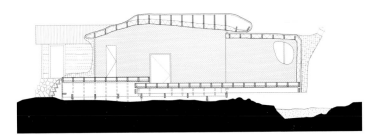

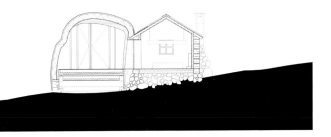

169

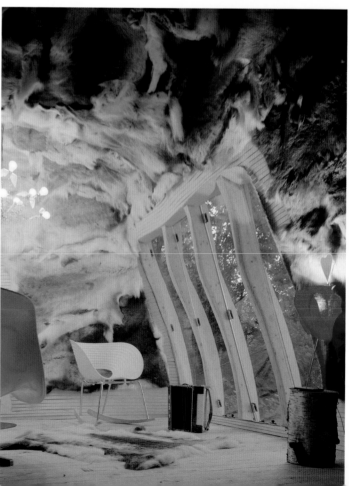

Structure axonometric

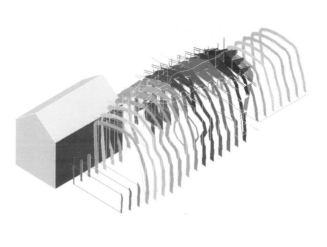

Construction details

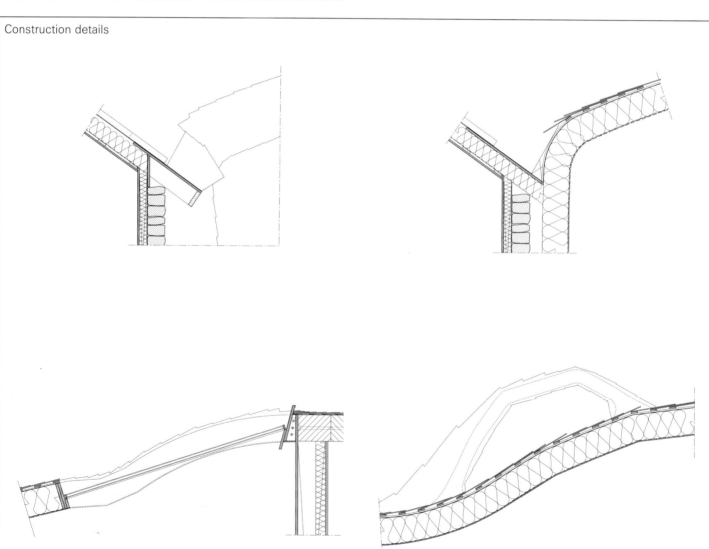

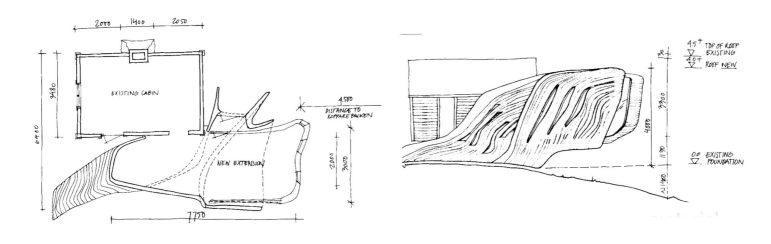

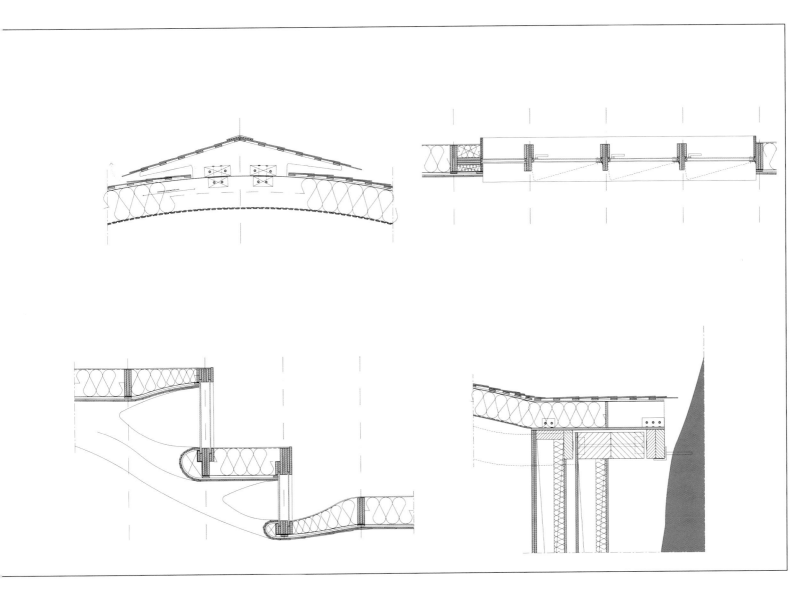

Rahel Belatchew Lerdell

Villa RBDVD

Photographs: James Silverman

Saltsjö-Boo, Sweden

RBDVD-house is a comment on the Swedish tradition of wooden single family houses where the highly standardized prefabricated industry has formed not only the construction process, but also the architectural expression. This wooden construction is characterized by a simple and clearly defined structure and space division where the proportions of the plan, the façade and the internal subdivisions are interrelated through repetitions and changes in scale of an initial rectangular form. RBDVD-house is situated in a residential area, high above street-level. The rocky nature of the site was decisive for the organization and orientation of the different rooms. The ground floor, facing north on one side and the rock on the other, provides room for the night (bedroom, bath, technique). An optimal exploitation of the surface and a maximum amount of light in the different rooms were the primary objectives. To achieve this, large windows are placed at the back, opening up to a view of rough stones illuminated by night. Likewise, the ceiling height, which is above standard, permits narrow passages which in themselves create a notion of space between two volumes rather than two walls. This is accentuated by lighting integrated into the wall between the bathroom and the passage. During the day, the translucent surface lets daylight pass through the building. At night, the illuminated wall brings daylight to the core of the house.

On the upper floor, one single room contains the kitchen and the living-room. Wide sliding windows at the back, to the south, open up the room to a large and sunny terrace. At the opposite side, facing the street, a long horizontal opening, like a slit, leaves at this height only the treetops to be seen, shutting out the neighbourhood. With a ceiling height of 3.5m, the upper floor contains a room within the room - a box in the box - in the shape of the kitchen which has its own lower ceiling detached from the rest. The lack of doors to the kitchen along with the bar counter running along the whole of its length, like the horizontal window in the living-room, opens to the north, creating an interaction between the bigger room and the smaller, the two only differing in scale. The relationship between the two creates an interface where spatial notions of isolated and integrated shift depending on the current activity, the lighting and the point of view. The cottage comprises two rectangular volumes (904 sqft): a larger communal dwelling complemented by an annex that virtually abuts it. Both volumes are designed as frames that allow light and space to stream through the open and extensively glazed long sides - timber casings of the cottage's functions and of the vistas that present themselves to the viewer looking through the house.

RBDVD-house is situated in a residential area, high above street-level. The rocky nature of the site was decisive for the organization and orientation of the different rooms. The ground floor, facing north on one side and the rock on the other, provides room for the night. An optimal exploitation of the surface and a maximum amount of light in the different rooms were the primary objectives.

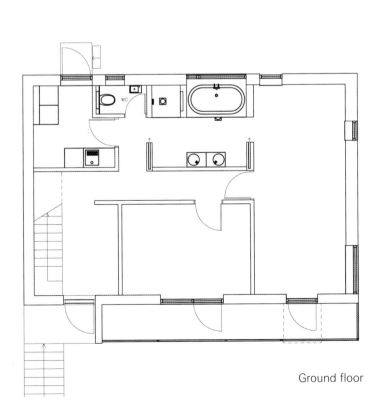

Ground floor

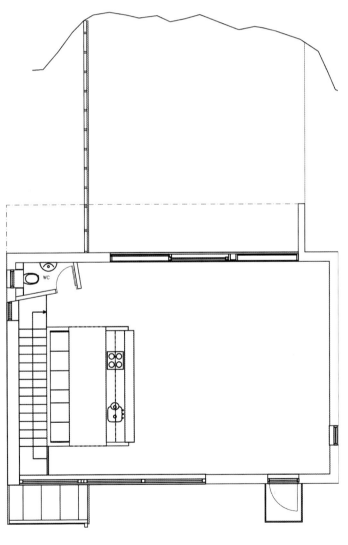

First floor

177

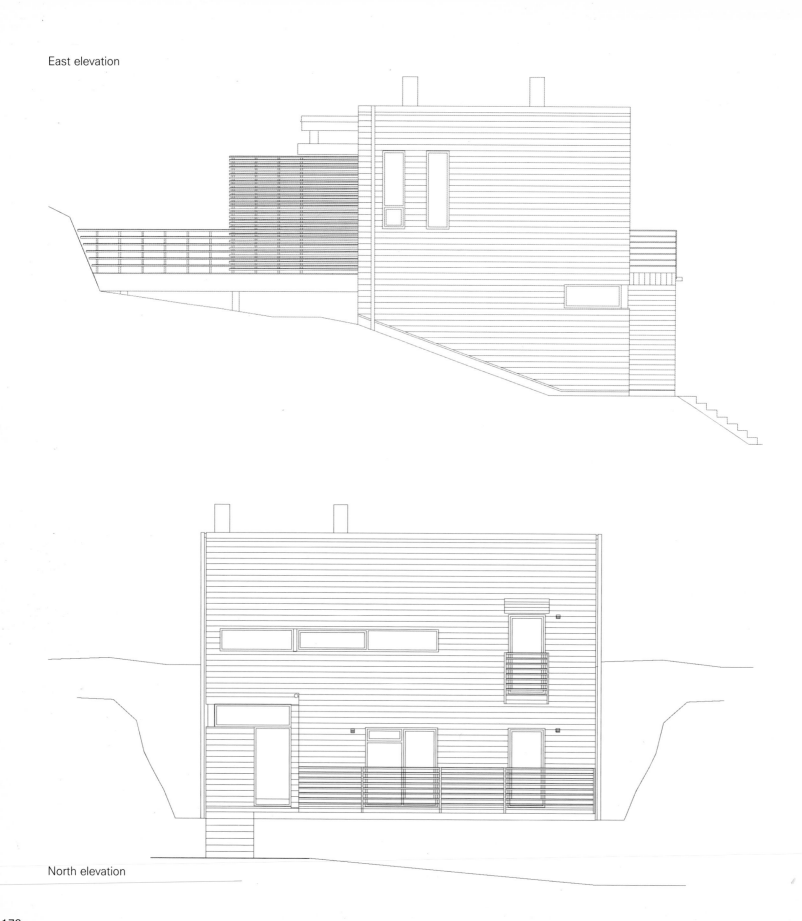

East elevation

North elevation